Hoaxes and Swindles

Richard Garrett
HOAXES AND SWINDLES

text illustrations by Edward Mortlemans

SEVERN HOUSE

First British hardcover edition published 1979 by
SEVERN HOUSE PUBLISHERS LTD
of 144-146 New Bond Street, London W1Y 9FD
with grateful acknowledgement to Pan Books Ltd

Copyright © Richard Garrett 1972

ISBN 0 7278 0418 9

Garrett, Richard
  Hoaxes and swindlers.
  1. Deception - History - Juvenile literature
  I. Title
  001.9'5'09   AZ999

ISBN 0-7278-0418-9

Printed in Great Britain by
The Anchor Press Ltd and bound by
Wm Brendon & Son Ltd, both of Tiptree, Essex

CONTENTS

Tread Carefully	7
The Man who Bought the Eiffel Tower	9
The Country that Never Was	23
The Abyssinian Affair	32
The Captain and the Mayor	43
The Loudspeakers that Lied	53
Interval: A Collection of Hoaxers	62
The Early Morning Men	77
The General	87
All Is not Gold	93
The Life and Death of Major Martin	104
The Improbable Paintings	117

You can fool all the people some of the time, and some of the people all of the time, but you cannot fool all the people all the time.

ABRAHAM LINCOLN

Tread Carefully

You are about to enter a strange world in which the people are not always what they seem to be, and in which deception produces fame and, sometimes, fortune. Here you will meet frauds and pranksters, and other characters who are not to be believed. Tread very carefully indeed: they are out to trick you.

Since impostors usually prefer to remain undetected, and since their victims seldom like to admit what fools they have been, the research for a book such as this is difficult. I have tried to make it as accurate as possible, but nothing of this nature can be the whole truth. Sometimes – notably when describing conversations – I have been compelled to use my imagination.

My thanks to the *Daily Mail* cutting library, back issues of *The Times*, *Grand Deception* (edited by Alexander Klein and published by Faber and Faber), *The Deceivers* by Egon Larsen (John Barker), *The Piltdown Forgery* by J. S. Weiner (Oxford University Press), *The Man Who Never Was* by Ewen Montagu (Evans Brothers) and *I Was Monty's Double* by M. E. Clifton James (Rider and Company). Without their help, I, too, would have been an impostor, for I would have had to invent all these stories.

R.G.

Tunbridge Wells,
1972.

1

The Man who Bought the Eiffel Tower

It was a beautiful morning in the early spring of 1925. Paris seemed to have thrown off her grey winter overcoat and slipped into something brighter. The trees in the street were already speckled with green. Overhead, the sky was a bright blue smeared with vestiges of cloud.

There was a kind of excitement in the air. It was the sort of thing one feels early on a fine morning, when the day has not yet been soiled by human comings and goings. Perhaps it would be fair to say that everything looked as if it were new.

André Poisson paid off his cab outside the Hotel Crillon and took a deep breath. He was wearing his best suit and a heavily starched shirt. He had to admit that he felt somewhat less than comfortable in it. What a pity, he told himself, that one needed to dress up for these meetings. He would have been much happier in the old and crumpled clothes that he wore for his day-to-day work as a scrap dealer.

But then he looked up at the imposing front of the hotel and corrected himself. Of *course* one should look smart when one came to such a place as this. For the umpteenth time, his fingers fondled the letter in his pocket. It was typed on thick paper, and was signed by the deputy director of the Ministry of Posts and Telegraphs. According to the writer, he was about to hear of a substantial business opportunity

... only a few, very select, dealers were being invited ... if he cared to be present at the conference room in the Hotel Crillon at 10.30 AM ... and so on.

A little nervously, he walked up the steps. These places always made him feel ill at ease. It was strange: when it came to negotiating a contract, few people were more shrewd – and, indeed, more tough – than André Poisson. But, just the same, these posh establishments disturbed him. Perhaps it was because he came from the provinces. His parents had been poor, and the large income he enjoyed nowadays was entirely due to his own efforts. He should be proud. He was more than a match for those flunkeys who seemed to regard him with such superior airs.

He went up to the man behind the hall porter's desk and asked: 'Where's the conference room?'

The man was checking some document. Without looking up, he started to say: 'If you will go up ...' but then, as he felt a substantial helping of francs nudge its way into his hand, he put down his pencil. 'One moment, Sir,' he said. 'I will have you escorted there.'

Poisson smiled to himself. There was nothing in this world which could not be bought – even respect from these jumped-up hotel servants.

The room was spacious with large windows overlooking the street. He was greeted at the door by a young man wearing a superb suit and with beautiful manners. 'Monsieur Poisson,' he said. 'How good of you to come. I am so glad you were able to make it. The deputy director will be here in a moment or two. Coffee is being served, or perhaps you would prefer a glass of wine?'

André Poisson said that coffee would suit him very well. One needed to keep a clear head on these occasions. A waiter handed him a cup and he glanced around the room.

There was a table in the middle with seven chairs around it. At each place, a pad of notepaper and a pencil had been thoughtfully provided. Apart from the young man, there

The Man who Bought the Eiffel Tower

were four other men present. He recognized two of them – Plevin from Neuilly and that rascal Girousse who had a small business somewhere on the road to Versailles. He thought that Plevin nodded in his direction, but he pretended not to see.

At that moment, the door opened and a tall, very distinguished looking man came in. He must have been in his mid-thirties; he was carrying a briefcase and wearing a black jacket with striped trousers. But the most impressive feature about him was his hands. Every gesture he made was so eloquent, that Poisson couldn't help feeling he would have made an excellent actor.

'Now, gentlemen,' the younger man was saying, 'if you would care to sit down, the deputy director of the Ministry has something he would like to say to you.'

When they had settled themselves, the tall man opened his briefcase, laid a number of documents on the table and carefully lit an expensive cigarette.

'You have already met my secretary,' he said. 'I am the deputy director of the Ministry of Posts and Telegraphs, and I should like to welcome you to this meeting. I must emphasize, gentlemen, that what I am going to tell you must be treated with the greatest confidence. Indeed, I should point out that, before we sent you your invitations, each one of you was very thoroughly investigated. The nature of my news is so important, such a matter of national concern, that only the most trustworthy, the most serious, the most scrupulous, businessmen in Paris are being let into my Ministry's little secret.'

He paused for a moment, and Poisson looked across the table at Girousse. The dealer seemed to be puffing his chest out with pride. 'Pompous devil,' he thought. 'Does he really imagine that these words apply to *him*?'

But the tall man was speaking again. Poisson noticed that he had the merest trace of a foreign accent, which seemed strange in a civil servant. Possibly he came from Alsace or somewhere like that. Up there, he believed, many people still spoke German.

'I imagine,' the man was saying, 'that you have all been reading your newspapers. It is unnecessary for me to tell you that the Eiffel Tower, one of the more noble features of our noble city, has fallen into a serious state of disrepair. If all the work which is urgently needed is carried out, the bill will run into hundreds of thousands of francs. More than any of us sitting round this table could afford and – dare I say it – more than France can afford.'

He then proceeded to give them a brief outline of the Tower's history: how it had been built by a civil engineer named Gustave Eiffel from an idea which had been approved by the authorities in 1886. The work was completed in March 1889, and, on the 31st of that month, the Tricolor was flown from the top for the first time. The Tower, which was 1,000 feet high, was constructed from iron; there were

18,038 different components
no fewer than 1,050,846 rivets holding them together,
and the whole thing weighed 7,175 tons.

'Just think of that, gentlemen,' the tall man said. 'Seven thousand one hundred and seventy-five tons of solid iron. Isn't that a scrap dealer's dream?'

There were murmurs of agreement, and one of the dealers laughed.

'Now, gentlemen,' the man said, 'we come to the reason for your visit here today. As I have already said, it must be treated with the utmost confidence, for the political ramifications are enormous. If the news were released at the wrong time, it might result in serious rioting – or even civil war. It is, and I emphasize this, as serious as that.'

He looked round the table: his sallow forehead wrinkled in a frown and his grave eyes seeming to command them to secrecy. Poisson was impressed. This man was no empty-

The Man who Bought the Eiffel Tower

headed Government employee, but an official of standing and, one imagined, power.

'I told you that it would cost hundreds of thousands of francs to repair the Eiffel Tower. That is more, I am bound to say, than we can afford. After a long and very earnest consideration of the question, the Government has decided that the problem has only one solution. Unless the Tower is repaired, it will fall down. The French Government has decided to *pull* it down.'

There was a sudden, deep, silence. It was as if the traffic outside had come to a standstill. The news was so fantastic, so unbelievable, that they all felt stunned. But, in the mind of André Poisson at any rate, business was never very far away. Over 7,000 tons of scrap iron – what a fortune could be made from that. A mountain of metal and all of it from the Eiffel Tower. The very history of the stuff would be sufficient to add to its value.

'You mean,' he heard himself saying, 'that we might be able to buy it?'

'The Eiffel Tower,' the man said, 'will go to the highest bidder. Under the unfortunate circumstances my Government feels that this is the only thing that can be done. Believe me, gentlemen, we have not come to this decision without a great deal of thought. We have considered every possible way of saving the Tower, but everything points to this one conclusion: the Eiffel Tower must go.'

'But surely,' said Plevin from across the table, 'if you can't afford to repair it, none of us could afford to buy it?'

The man smiled a cold kind of smile in which his eyes had no part. 'I think you will find,' he said, 'that it costs less to pull something down than it does to build it up. As for the value of the iron, we – and by that I mean, France – are at your mercy, gentlemen. Obviously we shall not concern ourselves with frivolous bids, but we should not expect such an attitude from the likes of you. You are, if I may say so, at the very summit of your profession. You are responsible businessmen. If you will let me have your offers in sealed envelopes by tomorrow morning, they will be carefully studied. Whoever submits the highest will receive the contract.'

He looked across to his secretary, who was sitting at the far end of the table. 'Have I forgotten anything?' he asked.

'Just one point, Sir,' the young man said. 'These gentlemen may be wondering where to send their communications.'

'To the Ministry of Posts and Telegraphs, I suppose,' Plevin said.

'Ah – no,' the tall man said. 'I'm glad this point has been brought up. Because this is so secret that not even underlings in my own department know about it, we are using this hotel as our headquarters for the deal. If you would be so good as to have them sent round here addressed to . . .' and he gave them a name that they all wrote down.

'And now,' he said, 'it occurred to us that you might care to come with us on a tour of the Eiffel Tower. All of you have obviously been there before, but this may help to refresh your memories. We have, I hope, a couple of taxis waiting outside.'

The restaurant on the Tower was shut, and the tall man said that he was sorry about this, for he would have liked to entertain the dealers to luncheon. But the lifts were working, and they went up to the top and saw Paris like a sea of greys and browns and glittering glass spread out beneath them. They stared for some time and with a kind of hunger at the complexity of girders, which needed to be repainted but otherwise appeared to be in tolerably good shape. For a large part of the exploration, André Poisson found himself in company of the tall official.

Although Poisson was uneasily aware that his companion was a member of the upper classes (he was sure that he had heard the secretary address him as 'Count' on a number of occasions), and despite the fact that, as he was only too often aware, he himself came from a much more humble family, in spite of these things, he found him strangely easy to talk to. Most people are fluent talkers and bad listeners. The tall official was different in this respect. He spoke well and convincingly and he always held your interest. But he was a good listener, too. He asked Poisson countless questions about his business, his home life, his childhood, and what his ambitions were. Poisson, who was inclined to be reserved, suddenly found that he enjoyed speaking about himself. He even confided the fact that, although he had made a good deal of money, he still felt unsure of himself.

'Not in the way of business,' he said. 'I reckon I'm shrewd and I can drive a very hard bargain. But – like at the hotel this morning – I don't feel at my ease. I'm happier in a small café with working-class chaps. Not, I suppose, that it really matters: if you've enough money, you can buy your way into society. Wouldn't you say that this was true?'

'Yes – I suppose it is. Fortunately, I have never had to. The pay of even a senior civil servant is not exactly princely, you know.'

'No,' said Poisson, 'I imagine not – but just think of the position you hold.'

His companion laughed. Stretching out an arm, he seemed to sweep the array of girders with his eloquent hand. 'What an exquisite design,' he said. 'Such a shame it must come down. But,' and he gave Poisson an understanding smile, 'one cannot help but be grateful that it will be put to good purpose. I am sure that your business would benefit considerably from such a deal?'

'We'd never look back,' Poisson said.

Back at his office, André Poisson did innumerable sums. The first thing was to consider what the bid ought to be, and the second was to decide how to raise the money. His bank account was well nourished and he always kept a large sum of

'What an exquisite design,' he said. 'Such a shame it must come down.'

The Man who Bought the Eiffel Tower

ready cash on the premises. But even these would only go a small way towards financing such a large deal. Still – it was by no means impossible. There were plenty of things that he could sell, and he could probably raise a mortgage on his house and on the scrapyard. Somehow, it could be done. In his mind's eye, he tried to imagine what the others might be offering, and then enlarged his own figure.

It was a business proposition, and yet it was more than a business proposition. To pull off such a transaction would give him fame, position, importance. He could just see the headlines in the Parisian newspapers. 'André Poisson – the Man Who Bought the Eiffel Tower.' Hall porters in expensive hotels would bow when he approached. Head waiters would regard him respectfully and obey his smallest wish. It would be the making of his business. It might also be the making of himself.

He took a piece of notepaper, and wrote 'Eiffel Tower' at the top. Then he began: 'I, André Poisson, trading under this name, have pleasure in offering for the above property ...' And then he crossed it out, crumpled up the paper, threw it away and started again. After several attempts, he got the wording to his liking, signed it, and sealed it up in an envelope. Not wishing to trust his clerk with such an important document, he ordered a taxi and delivered it to the Crillon Hotel personally.

The only thing to do now was to wait and hope.

That night, he found it hard to sleep. Was he, he asked himself, really doing the right thing? What if he could not find a market for so much scrap metal? He would be ruined – no doubt about that. Nor would he be able to find any sympathy anywhere. People would laugh at him. 'Poor old Poisson,' they'd say. 'Overreached himself. Thought he was on to the biggest deal in history, and now look at him. Silly old fool. Makes you laugh really, doesn't it.' Chortle, chortle, chortle.

Well – damn them – he'd make a go of it. He'd sweep up a huge profit off the floor. He'd be rewarded for being more courageous than all the rest. But suppose the people of Paris became angry at him for buying their beloved tower and pulling it down? As an act of protest they might refuse to purchase the iron. And that official – the Count (was he really a count, or had he misheard?): charming man. Polished, suave. Good talker, marvellous listener. But wasn't he a bit too smooth for a civil servant? The ones Poisson met in the way of business were not nearly such imposing characters, but then they were lower down the scale. They always wanted a sum of money to help the negotiations along. Not exactly bribes. Perhaps commission was a better word. But the tall chap had made no such suggestion. Possibly he was too important for that sort of thing.

The next morning, he went wearily about his business, waiting all the while for the telephone to ring. At about three o'clock in the afternoon, there was a knock on his door and his clerk came in. 'There's a gentleman to see you, Monsieur Poisson,' he said. 'He's from the Ministry of Posts and Telegraphs. I told him you were here.'

'Of course I'm here,' Poisson said. 'Bring him in at once. Do you want to keep a senior civil servant hanging about? What kind of people will he think we are?'

It was the secretary. He was in the best of humour, and he stretched his hand out. 'Monsieur Poisson,' he said. 'I want to be the first to congratulate you. A very shrewd bid, if I may say so. The deputy director is delighted. Once the formalities have been concluded, the Eiffel Tower will be all yours.'

'Heavens!' thought Poisson. 'I've done it!' 'Please sit down,' he said. And he offered the young man a cigarette from a crumpled packet that was lying on his desk.

But he was too old a campaigner to behave as a small child who has just been given a new toy. He gave a quick smile, and then he composed his face into what he thought to be a tough mask. 'I am very pleased about this,' he said. 'It is, of course, an unorthodox affair.'

'I'm not sure that I understand,' the secretary said.

'Sending the bid to the Crillon Hotel instead of to the Ministry. And you and the deputy director are by no means the usual run of civil servants. Quite out of the ordinary, in fact. A certain amount of trust and goodwill has been necessary to believe in your proposition.' ('That's right,' he told himself. 'Never seem to be too eager, you crafty old Poisson – you.')

'I can assure you that it's all entirely above board,' the secretary said – a little bit coldly, Poisson thought. 'On our part, we might ask: how can *you* raise the money?'

'There'll be no problem about that. You'll have it within a week. My word, my bond – you know?'

Nevertheless, when the secretary had gone, he still felt just a little bit uneasy. Something, he felt was missing from the transaction. It had all been *too* smooth. *Too* civilized. *Too* easy.

The phone call came an hour or two later. It was the secretary. 'There is just one small point that the deputy director would like to discuss with you,' he said. 'It's the merest formality, but it's something which must be done before we can sign the Eiffel Tower over to you. Could you possibly come over to the Crillon right away?'

André Poisson said that he could.

The scene this time was an expensive suite on the second floor. The deputy director was walking up and down, seeming to be ill at ease. Poisson was worried. Had something gone wrong? Had he, in some way, given offence? Perhaps all that talk about trust and goodwill had been passed on to the great man and had offended him. He fidgeted nervously with a bunch of keys in his trouser pocket.

'Monsieur Poisson,' the deputy director began, 'I am delighted. You made a very fair offer for the Tower – better, indeed, than those of your competitors. I should like to be able to give you my immediate assurance that, once you have produced your money, the Eiffel Tower will be yours. But there is just one other matter which seems to have escaped your attention.'

He lit a cigarette. Said nothing for a moment or two. And then looked at Poisson hard in the eyes. 'I am a civil servant,' he said. 'As I believe I told you when we visited the Tower, our salaries are not over generous. I shall not deny that this sometimes makes things a little bit difficult. We have our positions to keep up. We must dress well, entertain – sometimes lavishly, maintain, you might say, a good appearance. All this costs money. Because of these things, we have, in our service – well, I guess you might call it, a small tradition. When a deal has been concluded to the satisfaction of both parties, it is customary for one, yourself – for example, to make a small contribution to ... Am I making myself clear?'

Poisson felt an enormous sensation of relief. This man was now talking a language he understood. Even at the top, they needed their slices of commission. How deplorable that he had never brought the subject up. The man must think him an uncouth bumpkin, a person quite unused to dealing with officials in high places.

'Of course,' he said. 'I understand perfectly.'

How fortunate that he had come out with plenty of money on him. With as much finesse as he could manage, he took a thick wad of notes from his pocket.

'Deputy Director,' he said, 'might I ask you to accept this as a small gift. A little token of my gratitude ...'

'My dear fellow,' the man said. 'How good of you. It was distasteful to have to bring the matter up, but I am sure you understand.'

A few days later, André Poisson called again at the Crillon. He had with him a cheque drawn on the Banque de France for a very large sum of money. He handed it over to the deputy director in his suite: they drank champagne to celebrate the deal, and Poisson was handed a document which gave him full entitlement to the Eiffel Tower. It was an imposing affair, with a heavy seal at the bottom.

'When can I start to pull it down?' Poisson asked.

'It won't be long now,' he was told. 'Just give us a couple of weeks or so. We have to consider how best to break the news to the public. I'm sure you will agree that it is in your own interests that this should be done in the most appropriate manner. When all is ready, either my secretary or myself will give you a ring.'

That was the last Poisson ever saw of the deputy director of the Ministry of Posts and Telegraphs, or of his secretary. A month went by, and he heard nothing. When he rang up the Crillon, he was told that nobody of the name he'd been given had ever stayed there. Yes – they had received a count there the other week. Count Victor Lustig, who had stayed in one of the suites. He had a young man with him named Collins. Perhaps these were the gentlemen M'sieur was thinking about?

M'sieur was all too horribly aware that they were. He telephoned the Banque de France to stop his cheque, but, as he feared, it was far too late. Somebody had come in and cashed it on the following morning. André Poisson had been tricked. He faced financial ruin but, which was worse, he faced social ridicule as well. He *could* inform the Ministry of Posts and Telegraphs. Or, he could go to the police, or even tell the newspapers that they might warn others of this artful impostor, Count Victor Lustig, and his assistant. But, in the end, he decided to do nothing. It is bad enough to be a fool: it is even worse to let the world know about it.

By the time André Poisson discovered the fraud, 'Count' Victor Lustig and his assistant 'Dapper Dan' Collins were comfortably ensconced in one of the leading hotels of Vienna. Every day, they studied the French newspapers to see whether anything had been published about their exploit, but the papers said nothing.

'That's good,' Lustig said. 'It means that we can give things a year or two to cool off, and then do it all over again.'

And they did – but, this time, the victim told the authorities, and the story was well publicized. Lustig and Collins got away in time; but, as the former said, it was 'a pity. I enjoyed selling the Eiffel Tower.'

As for the unhappy Poisson, he might have taken comfort from the fact that there had been other victims before him, and would, no doubt, be more in the future. In the early 1920s, Nelson's Column in London had been 'sold' to an American for £6,000; and, in the same year that Poisson 'bought' the Eiffel Tower, the White House in Washington was 'leased' to a cattle rancher for 10,000 dollars, and an Australian very nearly 'purchased' the Statue of Liberty.

Lustig had been born in 1890 at a small town in Bohemia. After his business adventures involving the Eiffel Tower, he made North America the scene of his operations. In 1935, he was arrested in connexion with a forgery offence. Twelve years later, he died in prison.

2

The Country that Never Was

If you happen to be in the right place at the appropriate time, and if you bear a quite remarkable resemblance to somebody else, you may find that you have been anointed king. The chances are, one must admit, unlikely – but it has happened. The individual in question was a German citizen named Otto Wiltt.

In his time, Otto Wiltt had been all manner of things. For a while, he was employed as a deep-sea diver. Then he turned his talents to big-game hunting, with fortune-telling thrown in as a side line. By 1912, he was serving as a major in the Turkish Army. Presently, he was posted to Tirane, the capital of Albania, which was then under Turkish domination.

He had not been there long before friends told him that he might easily be mistaken for a Turkish Prince named Halim Eddin. It was said with approval, for he was obviously a nice man this Halim Eddin, and the Albanians badly wanted him as their king. After living with the idea for a while, Otto Wiltt decided that life might, perhaps, be more pleasant as sovereign of Albania than it was as a major in the Turkish forces. To the best of his knowledge, Halim Eddin was many miles away and – well, why not have a go?

And so it came to pass that, one fine morning, Otto Wiltt emerged from a fancy-dress shop in Tirane wearing a magnificent uniform with heavy gold epaulettes and looking every inch a monarch in the making. When he drove up to the 'seat of government' in a hired carriage, he was greeted with raptures by the people, who insisted that he should be crowned king at once. It all sounds rather like a fairy tale, but they were nothing if not impetuous.

By all accounts, the coronation of the man who was believed to be King Halim Eddin, but who thought of himself as King Otto I, was a hastily improvised affair. Before the day was over, a crown had been placed on his head and he was sitting, if rather uneasily, upon the throne.

Of course, it did not last for long. The news got back to Turkey. Prince Halim Eddin wanted to know what had been going on, and the Sultan had some rather harsh things to say about impromptu coronations. King Otto I was forced to make an instant abdication, get the hell out of Albania, and arrange a rapid return to his native Hamburg. Not that he felt any sense of defeat: for the rest of his days, he always referred to himself as King Otto I, and if anyone facetiously addressed him as 'Your Majesty', he took it very seriously.

To become a king, if only for a day or two, may be an achievement. To create a nation, and to keep the myth flourishing for the better part of nine years, is almost a work of genius. If you try to find Cuani on a modern atlas, you will be disappointed. Nor will it avail you if you seek it in the alternative spelling of Couani.

As a matter of fact, the place probably still exists as a small collection of mud huts and a few acres of swamp on the border of Brazil and French Guiana. At the end of the nineteenth century it was part of some territory involved in a nonsensical frontier dispute between France and Brazil. There were even some minor military skirmishes over it, though why anyone should have wanted the place is a complete mystery. At all events, in 1900, the two sides agreed that it had all been rather silly, and Cuani was handed over to Brazil.

The Country that Never Was

That might have been the end of the affair, if another, completely fictitious, version of this sad and swampy place had not already been implanted in the minds of a good many Europeans. It had all begun in 1895, when a young man named Jules Gross came to Paris and announced that he was President of the Independent Republic of Cuani. He was nothing of the kind, and nor was there any such Republic. Jules Gross came from Cayenne in French Guiana, and his only claim to distinction had been the post of honorary secretary to the local geographical society.

But he was a dreamer. He published an official journal on behalf of his so-called country, in which he issued orders and proclamations and printed lists of cabinet ministers and ambassadors. He dressed himself up in uniform, and when he appointed civil servants (the idea was that Cuani was to be governed from France) he encouraged them to buy their own ceremonial outfits. The trouble was that one or two of the more peacock-minded members of his entourage outdid him in splendour and had to be dismissed. Not that it mattered very much, for they probably never received any pay.

When Cuani was handed over to Brazil, Gross must have felt that his notion of a Government in exile had failed, and he vanished as mysteriously as he had come – possibly back to Cayenne, where he may have treated the geographical society to a series of lectures on contemporary life in Europe.

This brief fluttering of the Cuanian standard in Paris might have been dismissed as a prank. But what had been a matter of no importance assumed new dimensions with the arrival in the French capital of a man named Adolphe Brezet. Goodness knows where he came from. It may, just conceivably, have been Cuani, though this seems as unlikely as everything else about him. Indeed, the remarkable thing is that he reigned as an impostor for four years, brought a worried frown to the brows of at least four foreign ministers and nearly hoodwinked a syndicate of shrewd businessmen,

Jules Gross, alias the President of Couani

who ought to have known better, out of £160,000. He did all these things with a technique which was so imperfect that even a shabby confidence trickster would have disowned it. For example, whenever he visited England, he travelled under the name of the Duke of Beaufort – to whom he bore not the slightest resemblance and who, one must suppose, was peacefully immured in his stately home at Badminton, Gloucestershire. One might have imagined that the improbable joint residence of a Duke and the President of a South American republic in one and the same body would have occasioned comment. But nobody seems to have noticed.

Furthermore, Brezet had no great gift for accuracy. It was he who changed the spelling, whether by accident or design,

The Country that Never Was

from Cuani to Couani. He also announced that he had ousted Gross as President after a palace revolution back in 1892 – apparently unaware that his predecessor (if that is the right word) had been governing the 'Republic' from Paris as recently as 1900.

However, one has to credit Brezet with the fact that he really got things moving. He published a book on Couani. On the frontispiece, there was a coat of arms and the nation's motto, 'I will strive by reason or force'. There was a map on which thousands of square miles just inside Brazil were coloured in red, and were said to represent the Republic. Towns and cities which nobody had ever heard of were marked in, and there were symbols showing the probable locations of gold mines.

The text outlined the country's history. There had, it appeared, been seven presidents in all, and the country was ruled by a house of representatives with one hundred members. No matter who they were, their object had always been the same: *to get the place recognized.* 'Poor Couani,' Brezet wrote – and his tongue cannot have been completely in his cheek at the time, 'for all its rain, its flags, its orders, and its coats of arms, remains unrecognized by the nations.'

There was certainly plenty of rain to feed the worthless swamps out in South America, and there were plenty of flags waving and decorations blossoming in Europe. Gross had seen to the latter, when he instituted 'The Order of the Star of Couani'. He awarded it to his friends, the band of officials he had recruited, and to anyone else who might be useful.

Having published the book, Brezet applied himself to transforming the dream into reality. His father was named as his Chancellor of the Exchequer, and consuls were appointed in Madrid, Berlin and London. He himself ruled, as Gross had done, from Paris. He succeeded in persuading a group of French businessmen to promise a subscription of £100,000 for the development of the country. Unfortunately, whenever one or another suggested that it might be a good idea if they booked steamer passages and went to visit the place, Brezet always had to say: 'I am so sorry, my friend. I, too, want to go out there. How do you think I feel – having to lead my people from Paris? But, I am sorry to say, there is a political crisis at the moment. It is a small thing, but you know how hot-blooded people are about these things? I am told that the Army has everything under complete control. Soon we will go there, you and I – but, for the moment, please be patient.'

And the businessmen, strangely enough, *were* patient. Brezet, meanwhile, slogged on with his campaign for national recognition. He wrote letters to Edward VII, the Czar of Russia and the Emperor of Japan, seeking their help. At least two of them must have been impressed; for, during the Russo-Japanese war of 1904, both countries inquired about the possibility of ordering warships from Couanian shipyards. It was left to Brazil to inform them that there was no Couani, no shipyards, and they'd have to shop elsewhere for their men of war.

On a trip to Manchester (whether as the Duke of Beaufort or as the President of Couani is uncertain), Brezet spoke to local tradesmen about the country's opportunities for development. They became so excited by the idea that eventually Sir Edward Grey, the Foreign Secretary, had to warn them against sending out money and goods to a non-existent place.

And, in London, the suggestion of gold mines aroused a good deal of interest in the City.

Out in Couani, of course, the people knew nothing about the great campaign that was being waged in Europe. They sat at the entrances to their mud huts, regarded the almost incessant rain, and had no thoughts whatsoever about 'the struggle against foreign domination', which Brezet described in such high flown phrases.

But now, the idea was wearing thin. Edward Grey's

The Country that Never Was

discouraging advice to the Manchester traders had done little to help the myth, and nor had Brazil's flat denial about shipyards to the Governments of Russia and Japan.

The rot really developed early one morning in 1904, when a squad of Spanish policemen rapped on a door in Madrid. Beside it, a plate announced 'Couani Consul General'. Presently a man in pyjamas appeared.

'What is it?' he asked.

'You are the Couani Consul General – or that is what you *call* yourself?' the detective said.

'I am that official.'

'We have orders to arrest you, Senor.'

'But,' the man exclaimed, 'what am I supposed to have done? You cannot arrest the representative of a foreign power. Have you never heard of diplomatic immunity?'

'We know nothing about that, Senor,' the detective said. 'That is a matter for the Department of Foreign Affairs.'

'And where are you from?'

'We are from the fraud squad,' the detective said. 'You might like to go upstairs and put on some clothes before we take you away.'

A few days later, a similar dialogue was conducted in Berlin.

The rest of the world was more tolerant. Whatever Brezet's intentions may have been, he never succeeded in fleecing anyone. Even those French businessmen were never actually parted from their £100,000. Indeed, this may never have been his intention. He inherited a dream country from Gross and he let the dream grow until it took over his whole life. When, eventually, the card house which was Couani collapsed, he faded into obscurity and was never heard of again.

Perhaps, in some respects, he resembled a man who turned up in Canada over forty years later, and with a very different background. I shall call him 'X', for he has received more than enough publicity in his time, and he must be desperately sick of the whole affair.

According to his story, he had served in Britain during World War II. At some point, he volunteered for training as a special agent. After he had completed his course, he was dressed in rags and dropped by parachute over France. For the next four years, he lived in a small community, posing as the village idiot. During this period, he gathered important information about German Army movements, which he radioed back to the UK, and he also helped to blow up bridges and troop trains.

Eventually he was discovered and handed over to the Gestapo, who tortured him most horribly and, having failed to prise any information out of him, threw him into a concentration camp. On his return to Canada, he told people about his experiences, was invited to give lectures and broadcasts, and presently became the subject of a book.

The book was read by a former pilot in the Royal Canadian Air Force who had served with 'X' during the war. It was, he said, a pack of lies. The man had only served briefly in Britain and had never been parachuted into France. Nor, indeed, had he ever worked for the intelligence service.

The author was called to account. He explained that he had checked every detail and had been able to verify them all with one exception. There was no record of 'X's' name on the Intelligence files. But that, as he not unreasonably pointed out, might have been a clerical oversight.

Faced with this confrontation, 'X' admitted that he had made it all up, and that the episodes he had described so vividly had been the work of others. He had begun his hoax in an attempt to illustrate how much the human spirit could withstand – even under torture. And then the story had grown and grown, until it had overwhelmed him and he was almost believing it himself. But he had never made any money out of his lectures and broadcasts. Every cent had gone to charity.

When people heard about the truth, they forgave him and treated him with kindness. Whether Brezet received any sympathy when his mud-hut empire of Couani was sponged off the map is, perhaps, doubtful. But perhaps he never wished for any. One can imagine him spending the remainder of his days in gloomy exile: a recluse brooding about the glories that might have been, endlessly reading his book about Couani, and imagining the Russian and Japanese dreadnoughts being launched from the slipways of shipyards that never existed. One can see him as he dreamed on summer days of escorting King Edward VII to a review of the Couanian Army; or, in winter, of riding in a sleigh beside the Czar of all the Russians. Perhaps, on these occasions, he would think of himself as quietly dressed as befitted a man who had also been the Duke of Beaufort – with just the Star of Couani ribbon in his buttonhole to give a discreet reminder of his position as a world leader. Adolph Brezet may have been an impostor but, by heaven, he was a romantic.

3

The Abyssinian Affair

The scene on that February day of 1910 was a pattern of grey: the choppy waters of Weymouth Bay, the warships at anchor, and the pale grey sky, which looked as if it might suddenly unload a scattering of snow. It was all in remarkable contrast to the complexion of the Commander-in-Chief on board HMS *Dreadnought*. Seldom, if ever, had the face of that very senior naval officer been a more livid shade of red.

The enraged Admiral held up a signal which had just been handed to him by his Flag Lieutenant. In a voice which was loaded with menace, he asked: 'Who is responsible for this nonsense?'

'The Foreign Office, I believe – Sir,' the Flag Lieutenant told him.

'You've read it?'

'Yes, sir.'

'Foreign Office!' the Admiral sighed like the first gust of wind that ushers in a storm. 'Crowd of damned diplomatic do-gooders! Couldn't survive for five minutes without my warships to back 'em up. They send us this telegram, giving us about three hours' warning, telling us that a gang of Abyssinian princes want to see round the flagship. There's even some drivel about their having to lie down and face the east at sunset.'

'An Abyssinian custom, I expect.'

'If anyone thinks,' and now the Admiral's anger was about

The Abyssinian Affair

to be unleashed, 'that I shall permit a bunch of damned Arabs to lie down on *my* quarter-deck, they are very much mistaken.'

'I think, sir,' the Flag Lieutenant said, 'you will find that Abyssinia is in Africa.'

'Africa, Arabia – what the devil does it matter? They're all of 'em filthy. They'd make a shocking mess. Probably never had a bath in their lives.'

'They *are* princes, sir,' the Flag Lieutenant said. 'They no doubt have slaves to wash them. Nubian slaves, I shouldn't wonder. In any case, their prayer mats might provide a measure of protection.'

'What the deuce are prayer mats?' the Admiral barked.

'It's all part of the procedure, sir. The idea is that they turn towards Mecca and prostrate themselves on the ground. It has to do with religion.'

'I don't care what it has to do with. I'm not having it. Until those wretched fellows are off my ship, there won't be any sunset. Issue an order: sunset is postponed until further notice.'

'Very well, sir.'

'And another thing. How are we going to communicate with them? Who speaks Abyssinian on board this ship?'

'Nobody, sir – but I understand they're bringing an interpreter with them.'

'Just as well.'

The Admiral walked over to his desk and sat down. 'Abyssinians,' he muttered unhappily. 'You'd better tell the Royal Marines' bandmaster to mug up their national anthem. And what about flags? Have to fly their confounded standard, I suppose.'

'I don't believe we have an Abyssinian standard, sir,' the Flag Lieutenant said. 'But I did hear that the Zanzibar version is on board somewhere. Perhaps that would do?'

'Have to. Can't see it matters. All these damned Africans are alike. Can't tell one from another. They probably won't notice.' The Admiral rammed some tobacco into the bowl of his pipe and turned to the next item on his list of disasters. 'What about food?' he said. 'These native characters have odd diets, you know.'

'That may be something of a problem,' the Flag Lieutenant said. 'Possibly the interpreter will be able to make some suggestions.'

'Be too late by the time he arrives. Give 'em afternoon tea. Everybody drinks tea.'

'Yes, sir.'

'One more thing, Flags,' the Admiral said. 'You'd better meet the blighters at Weymouth Station. Must put on some sort of reception for them.'

'Very good, sir.'

The Flag Lieutenant saluted and went about his business.

At Paddington Station in London, the station master had already made up his mind that this was going to be a particularly awful day. He leaned forward in his chair and regarded his visitor with pleading, almost moist, eyes.

'But, Mr ... I'm sorry, I didn't catch your name,' he said.

'Cholmondeley,' the elegant young man said. 'Herbert Cholmondeley. It's pronounced "Chumley", but spelt C-h-o-l-m-o-n-d-e-l-e-y though heaven knows why.'

'Mr Chumley. You said you're from the Foreign Office?'

'My very words.'

'And you have to take these Abyssinian princes down to Weymouth?'

'Precisely.'

'And you require a special train for them?'

'Beautifully put.'

'Tell me, Mr Chumley,' the station master was now fidgeting nervously with his watch chain. 'Tell me, my good sir – have you any idea of how much time it takes to *arrange* a special train?'

The Abyssinian Affair

Herbert Cholmondeley smiled. 'No time at all, I'd imagine. The well known magic of the Great Western Railway. Miracle workers all, I expect.'

'Mis-ter Chum-lee – we are not miracle workers. You say they'll be here in less than an hour. We could hardly raise steam in a locomotive in that time. You must be reasonable.'

'The Foreign Office is always reasonable,' the young man said. 'That is the very purpose of our existence. But these are princes, my dear station master. Men of Royal Blood. They are guests of our country: visitors to His Majesty's combined Home and Atlantic Fleets. We can't treat them as if they were a trainload of trippers. What do you suggest?'

'I can put an extra coach on the eleven-thirty, and that's *all* I can do. I'm sorry. I'd like to arrange a Royal Train, but it just isn't possible. You *must* see my point of view.'

'Most clearly,' the young man said. 'An extra coach will have to suffice. And now – what about a reception committee?'

'You'll have to make do with myself, a ticket collector and half a dozen porters. I haven't anybody else available.'

'That should be ample. You'll wear your top hat, of course?'

'I *always* wear my top hat, Mr Chumley.' The station master got up and walked over to the door of his office. 'Hey – George,' he called. 'You'd better get out that red carpet.'

There were five in the party which the station master, in company with the urbane Mr Herbert Cholmondeley, one ticket collector and six porters, met on the station platform. Four of them were heavily bearded Africans – the fifth, who was introduced as their interpreter, spoke with a thick German accent. The princes varied in size from a tall man of athletic build, who seemed to be the senior member of the Royal party, down to a slender youngster whose whiskers came as a surprise. He seemed to be too young, or too effeminate, to grow any. But the station master was not going to worry himself over technicalities. He had done his best. The red carpet was out. The special coach had been added to the train within easy reach of the dining-car. It was now sufficient to utter a few suitable words of welcome on behalf of the Great Western Railway. The station master wasn't inclined to make speeches, and so he kept it short.

The interpreter gabbled a translation to the princes, and the princes gabbled back.

'Highnesses instrockt me to say – mist gretvull,' the interpreter said.

'Splendid. Quite splendid,' Cholmondeley beamed. 'And now we'd better be getting on board. Don't think the nation will not appreciate what you have done, Station Master. I know I speak for the Foreign Secretary, when I say ...'

But there was no knowing what he was about to utter on behalf of the minister. The princes and the interpreter had already climbed into the special coach, and he made haste to follow them.

Little of any note happened during the trip to Weymouth. Mr Cholmondeley and the German interpreter ate large luncheons, but the princes had nothing. Accustomed as they were to the strange ways of foreigners, this occasioned no comment among members of the dining-car's staff – though one of them was mildly surprised when, during the stop at Reading, the Foreign Office representative was seen to make a quick visit to the station buffet. He returned to the train with a number of bath buns clutched to his chest. Surely he and the German had already eaten their fill, or were these for the princes? One imagined that this type of confection was a rarity in Abyssinia. Perhaps it was the novelty that appealed to them.

Down at Weymouth, the Flag Lieutenant was on the platform to greet them and the local red carpet was given one of its rare glimpses of daylight. During the trip by car to the quay, and then in the Admiral's barge across the bay to the

*The Foreign Office representative returned to the train
clutching a bag of bath buns*

flagship, the princes seemed to be genial but lacking in conversation. When they said anything at all, it sounded like 'Bunga-Bunga' – a phrase which was obviously so unimportant, that the interpreter never bothered to translate it. For want of any better explanation, the Flag Lieutenant assumed that it was Abyssinian for 'Gosh!' or some other expression of delighted surprise.

As they came alongside *Dreadnought*, a guard of honour was lined up on the quarter deck, and the band of the Royal Marines went briskly into a rendering of the Zanzibar national anthem. If the princes noticed that it differed in a good many particulars from the Abyssinian melody, or if they observed that the wrong flag was flying in their honour, they were too polite to make any comment.

A rather calmer, but by no means contented, Admiral greeted them. He saluted and muttered something about 'Glad to have you aboard,' and the princes 'Bunga-bungaed' back.

'What they say?' the Admiral asked.

'Highnesses vish to bid walcombe,' the interpreter began. 'They say that in their country . . .'

'Yes, yes. To be sure. I daresay,' the Admiral cut in. 'Probably never seen a British warship before.' He turned to the Flag Lieutenant. 'Take 'em round the ship, Flags. Let 'em see whatever they want. I'll be in my dayroom if you need me.'

They explored nearly every inch of the vessel, from the gun turrets to the engine room, from the bridge to the mess decks. At every point, the princes 'Bunga-bungaed' delightedly, and Herbert Cholmondeley smiled happily upon his little flock. At tea in the ward room, he and the German ate well but, again, the princes took nothing.

'Something wrong with the menu?' the Flag Lieutenant asked – not without anxiety.

'Oh no – fine, perfectly splendid. Excellent baker you have on board,' Mr Cholmondeley said.

The Abyssinian Affair

'I mean about the princes. They don't seem to be eating or drinking anything.'

'Ah – there you have a point. Perhaps we should have warned you. In their country, they only take two meals a day. Very strict they are about it. Never touch more than two. If I might, perhaps, have just one more slice of that delicious cake.'

At some point during the meal, the chief staff officer came into the ward room. He had been ashore, and knew nothing about the royal visit. As he passed the interpreter, the latter fished the word 'Greetinks' from the back of his throat and received a blank stare in return.

'Come here, Flags,' the chief staff officer commanded.

'Sir?'

'Who the devil are these people?'

'Abyssinian princes,' the Flag Lieutenant said. 'The visit was arranged by the Foreign Office.'

'Yes, yes – I daresay. But that little fellow over there. The one who just spoke to me.'

'He's their interpreter. I believe he is German. Possibly there was nobody else available who could speak their language.'

'A German!' the chief staff officer fired the word with all the bark of a fifteen-inch gun. 'What are the fools at the Foreign Office thinking about? What is the Admiral thinking about? What are *you* thinking about, Flags? Has it occurred to any of you that HMS *Dreadnought* is one of the finest vessels in the Fleet? Can you imagine how much the German Emperor would give to find out about her secrets? And you, *all* of you, let a German interpreter have the run of the ship. It's tantamount to treason. I must have a word with the Admiral at once.'

At this moment, Herbert Cholmondeley, who had been hovering within earshot, interrupted their conversation. 'Sorry to butt in,' he said, 'but the sun appears to be going down. The princes will wish to make their devotions. Perhaps we should go on deck?'

The Flag Lieutenant was prepared for this. He caught the remark, as you might say, in mid-air, and neatly threw it back.

'The sun,' he said, 'only *appears* to be setting. It does not actually do so until the sunset bugle call has sounded. The sunset bugle, in a manner of speaking, makes it official.'

'I understand,' Mr Cholmondeley said. 'They should wait until they hear it? I'd better tell the interpreter.'

'That won't be necessary. They will not hear it. On the Admiral's instructions, the sun has been refused permission to set until further notice.'

'You mean, perhaps,' Mr Cholmondeley said, selecting his words with the care that became a diplomat, 'that it would be best if we now brought our visit to a close?'

'I mean exactly that. Their highnesses must be tired and, I shouldn't wonder, hungry. Furthermore, I understand that your coach is being attached to the six-thirty from Weymouth. There isn't too much time. It's been nice having you.'

Before embarking once more in the Admiral's barge, the senior prince fired a brisk burst of 'Bunga-bungas', and the interpreter converted them into 'Highnesses say 'sanks much. Royal Navy much good' which was only a small improvement on the Abyssinian version, but no doubt displayed a willingness to please.

On the way back to the shore, another naval launch went across their course in front of them. 'That fellow's going to be in trouble when he gets back,' the Flag Lieutenant said.

'Why's that?' Mr Cholmondeley asked.

'Crossed the bows of a vessel carrying royalty. Strictly forbidden – it's considered to be an act of discourtesy. Funny thing is that the chap on board's also royal. He's one of the Battenbergs, but he'll get hauled up on the mat just the same.'

The red carpet was still down on Weymouth platform, and a small crowd had collected. The princes and their escort

The Abyssinian Affair

embarked in their coach amid cheers, and settled themselves comfortably in their seats. The train was just pulling out of the station, when one of the princes sneezed. Mr Cholmondeley looked at him with concern.

'Tony,' he said, 'for God's sake, turn your face away from the window. Half your moustache has come off.'

On the following morning, the London newspapers published the story of this great hoax. Their readers, by and large, considered it to be the most amusing thing that had happened for a long time. On board HMS *Dreadnought* and in other warships in the Home and Atlantic Fleets, the atmosphere was explosive. There were even, it was said, fears that, if the Admiral went too close to the powder magazine, HMS *Dreadnought* might erupt in a sheet of flame, an ear-splitting bang, and a column of smoke.

The perpetrator of the affair was the young gentleman who played the part of Mr Herbert Cholmondeley of the Foreign Office. In real life, he was William Horace de Vere Cole, pastmaster of practical jokes and occasional impostor (though only for fun). Also in the cast were Anthony Buxton (he twice played cricket for Harrow against Eton and, in the hoax, performed the part of the senior prince), Duncan Grant (a famous painter), Guy Ridley (a judge's son), Miss Virginia Woolf (the famous novelist – it was she who impersonated the rather effeminate prince) and Miss Woolf's brother (the German interpreter). Afterwards, they were all roundly rebuked for their prank, though most people had to admire the efficiency and imagination with which it was executed.

The make-up was by William Clarkson who, in more serious vein, carried out this service for Mme Sarah Bernhardt and other famous professional entertainers. When asked by a reporter for his views on his craft, Mr Clarkson said: 'The greatest aid to disguise? Oh, the beard – certainly.' He also explained that the secret of success is never to attempt too much. Certainly, his work on the 'princes' was entirely convincing, though it had one unfortunate snag to it. It was quite all right, so long as they made no great attempts to eat anything. A bath bun taken after leaving Reading Station was all right. Anything more substantial was an open invitation to disaster.

The playing of the Zanzibar national anthem and the flying of that country's flag may not have passed entirely unnoticed; for, as we shall see in another chapter, Cole was fairly closely acquainted with certain aspects of that nation. Not that it would have worried him at all, for the princes' visiting cards, for want of an Abyssinian dictionary to furnish a translation, were printed in Swahili which is a totally different language.

4

The Captain and the Mayor

One day in 1906, Wilhelm Voight, an itinerant cobbler by trade, was released from a German prison. He was fifty-seven years old and, by his own reckoning, had spent at least half his life in gaol. His latest sentence had been a fifteen-year stretch for robbing the treasury of a law court in East Prussia.

There were many problems for Wilhelm Voight, and not the least of them was the fact that the authorities had taken away his passport and identity card. Without them, it might be said, he ceased to exist. It was difficult to travel; almost impossible to go abroad; and far from easy to find a job. By some means the situation had to be rectified.

When he had considered things for a while, he decided that, in his quest for an identity, he might also carry out a public service. In Germany at the time, the Kaiser was second only to God, the Army was second only to the Kaiser, and Government officials were only a short distance behind the military. What a wonderful thing it would be, he said to himself, if he could not only obtain a passport, but also hold the system up to ridicule.

He cannot have been a very clever criminal, for so many of his schemes failed and he nearly always ended up in gaol. On this occasion, however, he seemed to tap a stream of genius that he had never been aware of before. The ideas flooded into his mind, outrageously daring, brilliantly spectacular, certain to work. He studied his plan over and over again. Whichever way he looked at it, it seemed to be flawless.

The first requirement was a German officer's uniform. He decided to pose as a captain, which was senior enough to give him authority, but not so high and mighty that he would have difficulty in carrying it off. He found a complete outfit in a second-hand clothing store in Berlin. It was perfect: a little shabby, perhaps, but that was all to the good. If it were too smart, it might attract attention, and that was the last thing he wanted.

He put it on in front of a mirror; tried out one or two postures; and practised barking commands. He was a short man, but the uniform and the rigidly upright carriage he adopted made him seem taller. He clicked his heels, set his cap at a jaunty angle, and walked to the nearest barracks.

All that he needed now were a few soldiers.

Before very long, a corporal approached with a squad of five privates. Wilhelm Voight stepped out into the road. 'Corporal,' he snapped, 'where are you taking those men?'

'Back to barracks, sir,' the corporal replied.

'Turn them about and follow me. I have an urgent mission to perform on direct orders from the Kaiser himself.'

'Sir!' the corporal barked back obediently, and turned the men round.

They were marching towards a station on the Berlin circular railway, when they came across five more men. Voight halted his squad, ordered four of the newcomers to fall in at the rear, and sent the fifth man back to barracks.

When they reached the station platform, a train was just pulling out. With an authoritative bellow, Voight yelled: 'Stop that train and bring it back. I am commandeering it in the name of the Kaiser.' It was the sort of thing that, if you were an Army officer, you could get away with in the Berlin of those days. Like an obedient dog returning to its master,

The Captain and the Mayor

the train came backwards to the platform and stopped. Voight ordered the corporal and the nine privates into a second-class compartment. He helped himself to a first-class seat.

'Very well, Guard,' he said. 'You may go now.'

The train rattled off down the tracks. Everything, so far, was going beautifully to plan. Their destination was Köpenick, a small town on the outskirts of the German capital. The train stopped there, but Voight had decided to get out at a station about six miles up the line. It would, he considered, be more impressive if they marched the remainder of the distance.

When they had disembarked, the men were paraded and he inspected them. Magnificent! Their turn-out was a credit to the Fatherland. He really felt rather proud of his small command.

'Right,' he said to the corporal. 'Let's go.'

They marched for just short of two hours and presently came to the main street of the town. Outside the town hall, he halted the soldiers and told them to stand at ease.

'Listen carefully,' he said. 'These are your orders. I want you two men to commandeer a couple of cars in which to take our prisoners back to Berlin. You four men, go to the town's treasury, cut the telephone cables and wait for me there. The remainder of you will accompany me into the mayor's parlour. When we have finished, you will make your own ways back to barracks. Is that understood?'

'Understood, sir!' cried the corporal, almost choking himself with the speed and smartness of his response. And: 'You two men, take over those cars over there! You four – to the treasury, quick march!'

Taking his sword in his hand, Voight ran lightly up the steps to the mayor's parlour with the rest of the squad following. He brushed aside an inquiry from the commissionaire with a brusque 'Mind your own business,' flung the door of the parlour open, and strutted in.

The mayor, who was sitting at his desk, looked up with an expression of considerable alarm on his face.

'What is this?' he cried. 'What am I supposed to have done?'

'You are my prisoner by the Kaiser's orders, and you will be taken immediately to Berlin.'

'But I beg you...' the mayor began.

'You have nothing to beg,' Voight snapped. 'I have already told you that you are my prisoner.'

He turned to the soldiers. 'Take this man away,' he said. 'You may stop at his house and pick up his wife. After that, take him to headquarters.'

Once he had the room to himself, Voight turned his attention to his other mission. He had already made an ass of the mayor; he was in the process of making the Army look foolish; but he still had to find a passport and identity card. Somewhere in this room, he suspected, there must be both.

He searched swiftly and thoroughly, but could find neither. Perhaps they kept them at the treasury, he told himself.

The town treasury was only a few yards away from the mayor's parlour. He found the four soldiers waiting for him outside, and they reported that they had cut the telephone wires.

'Good,' Voight said. 'Now we shall visit the treasurer.'

They stormed into his office. Before he could so much as exclaim his astonishment, Voight had shouted: 'You are under arrest. I am ordered to take receipt of your funds.'

Rather feebly, the treasurer murmured something about needing to see his authority, but Voight barked back: 'I have no need of written authority. I represent the German Army, and I am under the Kaiser's orders. Can't you see that, you fool?'

The treasurer evidently saw it. Meekly he opened his safe

'You are my prisoner by the Kaiser's orders, and you will be taken immediately to Berlin.'

and took out a cash box. Placing the contents on his desk, he counted them out. The sum came to £200.

'Now make out a receipt and I will sign it,' Voight said.

The treasurer did as he was told, and Voight neatly penned a bogus signature at the foot of it.

'Excellent,' he said. Then, to the soldiers: 'Take this man – put him into the other car and drive him to headquarters. Make sure he doesn't escape. Right?'

'Right, Herr Captain,' one of the soldiers said. Looking the very picture of misery, the treasurer was led out of the building and chivvied into the car.

Voight searched everywhere for the passport and identity cards, but could find nothing. As it transpired, this part of his plan was doomed to failure from the very beginning. They did not keep supplies of these documents at Köpenick and never had done. However, he had accomplished a major portion of his grand design, and he was happy. All that remained was to put the final phase into effect. The mysterious captain, who had arrested the two leading citizens of this small town, now had to vanish – preferably without trace.

Before committing himself to his escapade, Wilhelm Voight had taken the precaution of leaving a parcel in the left luggage office of Köpenick station. It contained a suit of civilian clothes, shoes, a shirt and a necktie. The time had come to redeem it.

Fortunately, there were only a few people on the platform and nobody else in the public lavatory, where he discarded the disguise of the captain of Köpenick and resumed the identity of Wilhelm Voight, ex-jailbird and master impostor. He neatly parcelled up the uniform and tucked it under his arm. There was no way of concealing the sword, and so he left it behind.

He caught the next train back to Berlin and returned to his lodgings.

Poor Voight! It seemed that he had committed that rarest of misdeeds, the perfect crime. The newspapers grasped the story of his day's work at Köpenick with relish, and printed big stories about it. Whoever had been responsible for pricking the pomposity of the Army and local government officials was obviously going to become a national hero. Even the Kaiser, who might have been somewhat vexed by the performance, was heard to refer to the perpetrator as an 'amiable scoundrel'. The trouble was the police could find no clues to the culprit's identity.

Normally, this is a state of affairs that criminals find highly desirable. In this instance, however, Voight was rather less than pleased. It was as if an artist had made a magnificent painting, and had forgotten to sign it. Or as if

The Captain and the Mayor

an actor, playing the role of a lifetime, had found his name omitted from the programme. Voight was in the remarkable position of wanting to be arrested, for it was only by discovery that he could enjoy what he felt to be very well-deserved fame.

Eventually, he had to put the police on his own trail by planting a photograph in such a way that it would identify him as the bogus Army officer of the Köpenick raid. He was arrested at eight o'clock one morning, just as he was finishing a cup of coffee. One hundred pounds from the Köpenick treasury were still in his pocket book. He had already spent the remainder.

When he arrived at the police station, they presented him with a bottle of port.

His trial was a sensation. There were over ten thousand applications for admission, and most people thought the judge was rather harsh, when he sentenced Voight to four years in prison. However, he was not to serve all of it. The Kaiser, who turned out to have a much sharper sense of humour than most people had imagined, intervened and had it reduced to twenty months. He was released in 1908.

Until his death in 1922, Wilhelm Voight lived quietly and managed, for the most part, to stay out of trouble. In 1912, he made a brief comeback, when a Press Agency Report announced that he had died in hospital. Not without interest, he read his own obituary in the papers and was, by all accounts, well satisfied with it.

Wilhelm Voight died peacefully in his bed. In this respect, he was more fortunate than two Russian rascals named Odrinsky and Ragozin who, in 1933, were sentenced to be shot. It is hard to believe that they were entirely evil: or, indeed, that they did anyone grievous harm. Perhaps the truth about them was that they were unsuited to life in a Communist society. To this might be added the possibility that their imaginations were rather too energetic.

Odrinsky was described as a 'tradesman', though there is no knowing in what he traded. In public life, he masqueraded as a character named Evhenoff and told people that he was head of the Kara Sea Arctic Expedition. Accompanied by his friend Ragozin, who seems to have carried out his part in the deception under his own name, he related amazingly tall stories about how cold it was in the ice-clad regions of the north. Now and again, he would embark upon vivid descriptions of the wildlife, with particular references to awe-inspiring polar bears and comical sea-lions.

This must have been a redoubtable feat of the imagination; for, it later transpired, neither he nor Ragozin had ever seen a polar bear in their lives – not even in the Moscow zoo.

With a faked telegram, which purported to have been signed by the famous Russian polar explorer, Professor Samoilovich, as their only credential, the two men invaded the Moscow ministries. Under the pretext of raising equipment for their next expedition, they drew considerable quantities of goods from the People's Commissariat for Light Industry and the People's Commissariat for Supply. They also, and this must have required a tremendous amount of guile, won over the cooperation of the head men in the Office for the North, which was the branch of the Russian civil service concerned with Arctic exploration, research and communications.

Over a period of time, they obtained greatcoats, stoves, two complete sets of cinema equipment and (their greatest achievement) fresh sets of clothing for the entire crew of an icebreaker.

Since they were obviously unable to make use of all these things themselves, they must have sold them to other citizens, and this may be how their description as 'traders' came about. As an exercise in beating the system, it was on a far larger scale than Wilhelm Voight's hoax and, one supposes, considerably more profitable. Indeed, the very fact that they were able to maintain it for so long is a miracle. In Russia, the system was, and probably still is, everything. A man could scarcely breathe without the correct permit, but somehow Odrinsky and Ragozin talked and charmed their way through the barriers; told their very tall stories; and came away with even more loot. At no time did anyone seem to question their authority nor doubt their exploits.

Alas – in the end, the very bureaucracy which they cheated with such skill was their undoing. It was not an outrageous request, a demand for something impossibly big, that overthrew them, but a tiny little detail. A thing so small that it was not worth quibbling about. Odrinsky had been to the theatre. When the performance was over, he called at the cloakroom to collect his galoshes. By some oversight, the attendant had given him the wrong ticket.

If he had dismissed the matter and walked away, he and Ragozin would have lived to spin other yarns and collect more merchandise. Instead, he made a fatal mistake. He argued. He insisted that the matter should be put to rights: that he should be given his own galoshes and nobody else's.

Nothing is ever simple. The girl in the cloakroom refused to return them to him unless he filled in a form. Among the items that had to be completed were details of his place of employment. It then became necessary to check with this establishment that he was entitled to receive his rightful galoshes. Heaven knows what organization Odrinsky put down, but it was bound to be bogus. The cumbersome state machinery went into action and, once it had started, nothing could stop it. The inquiries covered a considerable field and, presently, the whole deception was unmasked.

The Kaiser may have been able to laugh at Wilhelm Voight's offence. The Soviet autocrats saw nothing funny in the frauds perpetrated by Odrinsky and his friend. They were sent to prison and the sentence of death was duly carried out.

5

The Loudspeakers that Lied

Today we have become quite accustomed to the power of radio and television. Nobody can fool *us*. Let them put impostors on the air. Let them try to mislead us. We shall just smile and drink our cocoa and (possibly) yawn. The last great TV hoax was a length of film screened some years ago at the end of a Monday night Panorama programme. It showed farm workers in Italy picking the 'spaghetti harvest'. The date, appropriately, was April 1st.

Most people know that spaghetti is manufactured in factories from wheat and water and goodness knows what else. Nevertheless, the shots of men and women cutting it down from the branches of trees had quite a number of viewers dismayed. Was it possible, they wondered, that they had been wrong about spaghetti? Were all the tales they had been told, were all the lists of ingredients on the packets, were all these things false? Seeing, after all, was supposed to be believing.

We now know that cameras can lie as adeptly as any confidence trickster. For much longer, we have realized that the spoken word may very well be untrue, and often is. But the word, when it comes over the radio, carries more authority. People have always been inclined to believe it, without realizing that radio can be one of the biggest liars, the greatest impostor, of them all.

Sometimes this happens unintentionally. There was, for example, an evening in 1926, when Londoners turned on their wireless sets and received the shock of their lives. They had missed the introduction, but there was no doubt at all about the subject. The smooth, precise, voice of the announcer was reporting terrible happenings. The nation, it appeared, was in a state of revolution. Mobs were marching down Whitehall: some were attacking the Houses of Parliament, other rioters were attempting to blow up the Savoy Hotel. It never occurred to many of these listeners that the situation was other than as described. Afterwards it was estimated that something like 20,000 letters and telephone calls were received from people who had been brought close to panic by the programme.

Had they heard the opening announcement, they would have known that it was all fictitious: that the 'announcer' was no ordinary newscaster, but a celebrated Roman Catholic priest named Ronald Knox. In addition to his religious duties, Monsignor Knox was a writer who enjoyed literary jokes. On this occasion, he had the public almost completely fooled. It may not have been his intention, but it was dangerously successful.

Circumstances, admittedly, were on his side. Nineteen twenty-six was the year of the General Strike. It was a period of enormous industrial unrest, when an army of white-collared citizens enlisted as special constables to quell riots which were anticipated but never came. The Knox broadcast gave an all too vivid picture of what might have happened.

Nineteen years later, in 1945, the first atom bombs were exploded. In the following year, panic swept across France, when a programme entitled *Platform 70* was broadcast from Paris. According to the story line, an uncontrolled wave of atomic energy had thrown the Atlantic Ocean into a condition of turmoil, and the terrible tide of destruction was now sweeping across France towards the French capital. Two listeners died from terror: thousands of others had to be calmed down by announcements, repeated at short intervals, reassuring them that it was all make-believe. Squads of police

The Loudspeakers that Lied

cars were mobilized – to patrol the streets and to issue the information through their loudspeakers.

In May 1947, listeners to the American Armed Forces Radio Station in Tokyo received a shock which was very nearly as bad. The time was seven o'clock in the evening. An announcer interrupted the programme to report that an 'unidentifiable sea monster', at least twenty feet long, had come ashore at a point somewhere between Tokyo and Yokohama, and was terrorizing the local inhabitants. 'Stay tuned to this station for further announcements,' the broadcaster advised.

At five-minute intervals, he chipped in with more news, and all of it was disturbing. Allied troops were warned to keep off the Tokyo streets, since the monster, with an uncanny sense of direction, appeared to be on course for the Japanese capital. A southbound train from the city was said to have been attacked by the creature and derailed. 'Casualties,' the announcer told his listeners, 'are not yet known.'

But the armed forces, if one was to believe the reports, were fighting back. One skirmish involved a party of soldiers with a flame-gun. Possibly the monster had a fireproof skin. At all events, it was said to have got the best of the encounter.

Japanese citizens, sitting by their radio sets, believed every word of it. More surprisingly, many of the American Army men turned out to be equally credulous, and this included the military police. One colonel, having heard the news, made a rapid departure from a dinner party. Back at his base, he assembled a flying column of three trucks crammed with soldiers and two jeeps with machine guns mounted on them. Taking his seat in the leading vehicle, he ordered the driver to take the road to Yokohama.

'We'll get this monster or bust,' he said – or something like that.

The report of the train episode had people really worried, and the officials at the radio station must have felt that the joke had gone far enough. At eight o'clock, the announcer

The American Armed Forces fight back

The Loudspeakers that Lied

told his anxious audience that it had all been conceived in fun: that there was no monster and the railway had suffered no damage whatsoever. It had all been a happy little hoax to celebrate the radio unit's fifth birthday.

Many people, including one irate colonel and his detachment of men, felt that the joke had badly misfired. However, as the producer remarked afterwards, you can't please all the people all the time, any more than you can fool them all the time.

The trouble, of course, is that the listening public is very apt to jump to conclusions long before it has grasped all the facts. A fine example of this occurred in 1955, when Scandinavian countries were horrified to hear of an earthquake which had shaken Portugal and caused fearful devastation in Lisbon. Had they heard the beginning of the programme, they would have known that, though the information was correct and 30,000 people had been killed, the disaster had occurred two hundred years previously. It was an historical programme which had been up-dated by an opening announcement to the effect that: 'We now interrupt this programme to broadcast an extra news bulletin.'

In some respects, it was similar to a broadcast seventeen years earlier, which had brought panic to parts of North America, and which can reasonably be summed up as the day the Martians invaded the USA.

Strangely enough, the great drama of the men from Mars would probably have never happened, had it not been for a very popular ventriloquist and a considerably less popular singer. The date was Sunday, October 30th, 1938, and the time: 8 PM. By a pure coincidence, it was Hallow'een.

In a studio belonging to the Columbia Broadcasting System in mid-town Manhattan, a party of actors belonging to Orson Welles' 'Mercury Theatre of the Air' was about to broadcast an adaptation of H. G. Wells' novel *The War of the Worlds*. It was during a period of considerable tension.

One month earlier, the British Prime Minister, Neville Chamberlain, had made a flying visit to Munich. After talks with Hitler, he achieved an agreement which helped to postpone the outbreak of World War II by just short of a year.

Those who had been waiting for the troops to march and the guns to fire and the bombs to explode, felt relieved. The prospect of a new war seemed rather like an invitation to the end of the world. But this poor old planet had been reprieved – at least, for the time being. Nevertheless, there was still a good deal of uneasiness. The public in Europe and North America had become conditioned to expect the worst.

The production which Orson Welles and his players were about to enact was not expected to be up to much. A secretary employed by the unit had dismissed it as 'silly', and a studio technician had called it 'dull'. At some point in rehearsal, they even considered doing something else; but the only possible alternative was *Lorna Doone*, and that, they decided, would be even duller.

As for the majority of American listeners, they preferred to tune their sets to another station, where a ventriloquist named Edgar Bergen and his dummy, an amusing puppet named 'Charlie McCarthy', seemed likely to be much more fun. Bergen was at the height of his fame, and pollsters estimated that about thirty per cent of the listeners switched on to his programme – against only three per cent who wished to hear *The War of the Worlds*.

Five minutes after the latter had started, Edgar Bergen's performance came to an end. A rather mediocre singer, who featured well down in the charts, took over. A good many listeners grunted something about not wanting to hear *him*, and re-tuned their sets. *The War of The Worlds* was now five minutes old, and they had missed the opening announcement that 'The Columbia Broadcasting System and its affiliated stations present Orson Welles and the Mercury Theatre of the Air in *The War of the Worlds* by H. G. Wells.'

The Loudspeakers that Lied

Even those who had heard the beginning were in for surprises, and those who had read the book must have found the beginning no less disconcerting. Wells' story is set in the Home Counties. At first it is thought that a meteorite has come to earth near Woking in Surrey. But then it is seen to be a metal cylinder inhabited by unpleasant creatures looking rather like octopuses. The visitors advance on London and create havoc and death before they are slain – not by guns or by flamethrowers, but by bacteria. Systems which had turned out to be impregnable to weapons are destroyed by a bug which was not identified by the author, but which could have been an ordinary flu germ.

In Orson Welles' adaptation the scene was set at Grovers Mill, New Jersey, with New York City as the Martians' eventual target. H. G. Wells told his tale as a straightforward narrative, describing the events from the point of view of one character. Orson Welles' handling of the story was very different.

After the announcement of the programme, a weather forecast was given, and then listeners were told that dance tunes would be relayed from a New York hotel. Suddenly, the music was interrupted by a quick-fire news flash about the invasion from Mars. The rest of the play was narrated by this technique. It was brilliantly done – so brilliantly that the newscasts were a little too realistic. Police telephone switchboards were suddenly flooded with calls from panic-stricken citizens asking for advice.

A report that the invaders were using poison gas caused twenty families from a block of houses in the New Jersey town of Newark to come running out into the street, wet handkerchiefs over their heads and with towels covering their faces. There were more phone calls to the police, asking such questions as 'Are any gas masks available?' and 'Ought I to close my windows?'

In Riverside Drive, New York, something like one hundred people evacuated their homes in readiness for flight;

and, in Providence, Rhode Island, all the lights were switched off to confuse the invaders. In Pittsburgh, a woman tried to poison herself, preferring this kind of death to destruction by the Martians. In Harlem, 'end of the world' prayer meetings were held; a labourer living somewhere in Massachusetts spent all his savings in an attempt to buy his way to safety; at least one man in San Francisco volunteered for the American armed forces; and, way down south in Birmingham, Alabama, the inhabitants gathered together in churches to pray for deliverance from the fearful creatures with leathery skins and death-dealing tentacles.

But, almost as bad, was the second wave of rumours which this fantastic impostor of a broadcast provoked. There were stories of masses of people who, attempting to make a getaway in their cars, were spinning off the roads and choking the ditches. There were tales of the inhabitants of apartment houses moving their furniture into the streets, and even accounts of solid citizens in the Middle-West fleeing to the hills and hiding up in caves. These were all untrue, and were not even features of the play. Popular imagination had gone berserk, and there was no knowing where it all might end.

Halfway through the programme, which only lasted about an hour, there was the announcement that: 'You are listening to the CBS presentation of Orson Welles and the Mercury Theatre of the Air in an original dramatization of *The War of the Worlds* by H. G. Wells. The performance will continue after a brief intermission.' But it came too late. By this time, many listeners had been dislodged from their radio sets by the tide of panic, and the words were spoken to empty rooms.

Eventually, after countless soothing announcements, the truth got through. America, rather shamefacedly and, in some instances, very angrily, went home. The panic was over. The invaders who never came had departed. All was as well as it could be in a nervous world.

But those citizens of the USA who were hoaxed by this all

The Loudspeakers that Lied

too vivid broadcast were not alone. When, in the following year, an adaptation of the programme was broadcast in Ecuador under the title of *The Men from Mars*, it caused a similar panic. In spite of rumours to the contrary, the only casualty in the United States incident was one young woman, who fell and broke her arm when running downstairs. In Ecuador, where they are presumably more excitable, a mob of indignant listeners burned down the radio station afterwards, and six members of the cast died in the flames.

The aftermath so far as Orson Welles was concerned was by no means bad. Thousands of people threatened to sue Mercury Theatre of the Air; but, after CBS had made a public apology, it all simmered down. Only one claim was made, and that was promptly settled. It amounted to three dollars twenty-five cents for a pair of size nine shoes. It came from that labourer living in Massachusetts, who had spent his not very substantial savings on a railway ticket to safety.

Welles and his Mercury Theatre were well rewarded. For some while they had been performing their weekly plays without a sponsor – a situation which, in the broadcasting world of North America, is tantamount to economic disaster. On the strength of *The War of the Worlds*, a leading soup manufacturer gave them a contract valued at a great many dollars.

But perhaps the biggest impostors in this remarkable episode were the creatures from Mars. As studies of the planet have since shown, it is a barren assembly of sand and rocks, swept by gales and apparently unable to support life of any kind. Certainly it could never be the home of intelligent monsters such as Wells invented, who may have been unprotected against the ravages of common germs, but who were supposed to be much more advanced scientifically than anyone on earth.

Interval

A Collection of Hoaxers

This is not a practical handbook for would-be impostors. If you wish to become one, you must work out your own tricks. And, if you are caught, you will oblige me by not mentioning this collection of stories. I want no part in the affair.

However, since we are dealing with this subject, we may as well do it thoroughly. As you will no doubt have observed, we have reached the halfway point. The stories will continue in a few pages' time. For the moment, I must ask you to consider some of the smaller items in my collection. Unlike most of the events reported elsewhere in the book, these were done without thought of personal gain. Their perpetrators merely wanted to have fun.

One of the most simple and beautiful practical jokes ever performed was the brain child of that prince of pranksters, William Horace de Vere Cole (he who arranged the visit of 'Abyssinian' royalty to the Home Fleet in 1910 which I have described in Chapter 3). Armed with a ball of string, Cole went up to a man in a London street and said: 'Excuse me, sir. I am carrying out some survey work. Would you mind holding the end of this piece of string for a moment, while I take some measurements?'

The man said that he would be happy to oblige. Cole handed him the string, unwound it, and vanished round a corner. He then raised his hat to another pedestrian and repeated the question. The man agreed. Cole thanked him and made off.

Interval: A Collection of Hoaxers

Goodness knows how long the two victims were left holding the string. It may have been for hours, though one doubts it. Cole was unable to enjoy their embarrassment; but he may have congratulated himself that, for sheer neatness, he had created the very model of a model practical joke.

Rather more elaborate in Cole's catalogue of handsome hoaxes was a type of joke which seems to be rare these days – taking up the road. Early one morning, he arrived in Piccadilly dressed as a navvy. He spent several hours digging a large hole in the centre of the street. Then he walked off.

Nobody questioned him, and the hole remained for several days before the local council decided that it might be a good idea to fill it in.

Some while later, a party of Oxford undergraduates moved in on Oxford Street. By the end of the day, they had taken up a hundred yards of roadway without being challenged. At the time, it seemed to be a record, but it was not to stand for very long. A few weeks later, a rival party toiled away for six days, excavating Throgmorton Street in the City of London. Nobody, at any time, asked to see their credentials. And, once they had departed, another ten days elapsed before a representative from the City Surveyor's department came along to investigate.

But these things happened many years ago, when roads were built from wooden blocks and were much easier to take to pieces. Nowadays, you would need a pneumatic drill, a compressor and heaven knows what else.

On the other hand, it *is* possible, if not to take up roads, then at least to produce the *threat* of doing so. An excellent example of this is the series of strange events which occurred one morning in the Yorkshire village of Hetton. This is a very pretty place which, tucked away in the Dales, seems to have slept soundly through the centuries. Neither the dreams of a property tycoon nor the ravages of an industrialist have disturbed its seasoned appearance, which dates back to the Middle Ages.

On this day, however, the inhabitants were in for a shock. There were *strange* men in the village. Some were busy with poles and theodolites and the rest of surveyors' paraphernalia. Others were handing out official notices to the residents. It seemed that the Government proposed to build a new road right through the middle of Hetton. It was to be known as the 'Dales Relief Motorway'.

But, the document made clear, the village was not to be ruthlessly bulldozed out of existence. Oh dear no – the Government was sensitive to its antiquity, and had agreed that it must be preserved. Rather than knock it down, they proposed to *move* it. Stone by stone, slate by slate, lock, stock and proverbial barrel, Hetton was to be shifted to a new site three-quarters of a mile away.

A wave of something not far from terror went from house to house. Was this really to happen? How could anyone actually move a village? And how would the inhabitants live while this extraordinary operation was taking place?

Governments sometimes did stupid things – but *this*!

A few hours later, after a considerable outcry, the matter was cleared up. The local county council knew nothing about it, and nor did Whitehall. It was all an elaborate practical joke, staged by students of Leeds University as part of their rag week. Nowadays, the villagers of Hetton laugh about it; but, during those grim hours, the prospect seemed horribly real and totally unfunny.

If there were a Horace Cole Award for the Best Prank of the Year (perhaps there *should* be, now that one comes to think of it), these students would certainly have won it, for this was an idea after the maestro's own heart. Although some of his best tricks were extremely simple, he was never afraid to stage something really elaborate. Consider, for instance, the time when he was an undergraduate at Cambridge. One morning, when reading his newspaper, he noticed that the Sultan of Zanzibar was paying an official visit to London. Something in Cole's mind lit up. The signal

Interval: A Collection of Hoaxers

was unmistakably clear: would it not, surely, be amusing if the Sultan were to include Cambridge in his itinerary?

Not wishing to bother the ruler, he decided to take his place. From London, he sent telegrams to the university and civic authorities, telling them to make suitable preparations for a royal visit. Then, carefully disguised and with a few friends playing the parts of aides and servants, he set off by train to the university town. The mayor and members of the corporation were at the station to greet him. There were polite speeches of welcome. Then he was handed over to the academic authorities, who took him on a tour of the colleges and entertained him as became his high rank.

During the trip, by an amusing irony, he was shown his own quarters. 'These are Mr Cole's rooms,' his guide explained. 'He's away in London at the moment, but I'm sure he won't mind.'

Not wishing to court discovery by making a return trip to London, he and his retinue vanished at some point during the afternoon. They were never seen (in their Zanzibar disguises) again.

Or: consider the case of Cole and the Prime Minister. By a strange quirk of fate, the former bore a remarkable outward resemblance to Ramsay MacDonald, the man who reigned as Britain's first Labour Prime Minister in the years between the two wars.

One evening during his first term of office, MacDonald had an appointment to address a gathering of trade unionists in London. He hired a cab to take him to the meeting and soon discovered that the driver was a very dull sort of fellow. He seemed to have difficulty in getting his vehicle to start. After that, he took all manner of wrong turnings and eventually arrived at the hall half an hour late.

Meanwhile ...

The trade unionists had settled themselves comfortably in their seats, and were looking forward to a thoroughly agreeable evening. Since their guest was a socialist of long standing, there was no doubt that his message would be sheer music to them. It would almost certainly deal with the struggle of workers against employers and kindred radical topics.

There was a scuffle of feet and MacDonald, or so he seemed to be, was escorted on to the platform. The audience waited, respectfully silent. The speaker flashed them a quick smile, cleared his throat, and began.

'Friends,' he said in that rolling Scottish accent which was Ramsay MacDonald's trade mark, 'let me tell you that the trouble with this country today is that wages are too *high*; working hours are too *short*; and profits for the employers are too *low*.'

The trade unionists sat stunned. This was the most abject heresy: words that any labour leader worthy of the name would die rather than utter. They could not believe that they had heard him correctly and then, suddenly, they noticed that he had gone. There was a scraping of chairs and an indignant babble of talk before, a few minutes later, the real Ramsay MacDonald arrived.

They had been entertained (if that is the right word) by Horace Cole, while one of his friends, masquerading as a taxi driver, had taken the real Prime Minister on a tour of London.

Cole seems to have had it in for politicians. He was once walking down a London street with a Member of Parliament, when he decided that his companion's conversation was becoming rather pompous. The man needed, Cole decided, to be taken down a peg or two.

He took his gold watch out of his pocket, and deftly slipped it into the politician's jacket. Then he said: 'You know, what we need is more exercise. I bet you a fiver that I can run faster than you to the next lamp post.'

Surprisingly, perhaps, the MP agreed. Cole gave the signal, and they set off. A policeman was on the far side of the street, and Cole suddenly yelled: 'Stop thief! Stop thief!'

Interval: A Collection of Hoaxers

The policeman hurried across, grabbed the Member of Parliament by his arm, and asked: 'What's all this, then?'

'This scoundrel,' Cole said, 'has stolen my watch.' And there, of course, it was – in his friend's pocket. The unfortunate man was taken to the nearest police station, where he was kept in custody for the better part of two hours before the matter was cleared up.

Jokes of this type are malicious. They are designed to embarrass and, at their best, they are very embarrassing indeed. Another example comes from New York and can best be described as 'The Affair of the Davenport'. A davenport, in case you are in doubt about it, is the American word for a large sofa (in Britain it is more commonly applied to small, ornamental, writing tables). It happened that, some years ago, a couple living in Greenwich Village had acquired one and were very proud of it. They had also, to set the situation correctly, engaged a new housemaid – and had been invited to a party by friends who lived on the far side of the street. These were the innocent raw materials of the joke: the men behind it were two humorous writers employed by the *New Yorker* magazine.

On the afternoon before the party, the two writers rang the bell of the house with the davenport. The maid opened the door, explained that her master and mistress were out, and asked what they wanted.

'We've come for the davenport,' one of the writers said.

The girl had no idea what they meant, but suggested they should help themselves. Moving into the drawing-room, they picked up the ungainly object, carried it out of the house, and across the street to the place where the party was to take place.

Again they rang the bell, and again a maid asked them what they wanted.

'We've brought the davenport,' the writers said.

With a slightly puzzled look, the maid said: 'You'd better put it in the drawing-room.'

The writers did that, and departed with happy smiles on their faces. Everything had gone beautifully to plan.

That evening the couple from what we may now call House A crossed the road to enjoy the hospitality of their friends in House B. You can, perhaps, imagine their dismay when, on entering the drawing-room, they saw fellow guests lounging about on their beloved davenport. To the best of my knowledge, the matter was never satisfactorily cleared up, and the inhabitants of House A lived in suspicion of their former friends in House B for the next several years.

Although magnificent when it comes off, this type of prank is elaborate, and requires a great deal of careful preparation. Had either of the couples been at home when the two writers called, the joke would have fallen flat on its face. It is certainly not something to be undertaken by the novice hoaxer. For him (or her), more simple exercises are recommended.

An excellent example is the case of a young man who once went into a café and ordered an ice cream soda. When it had been prepared, he said: 'Thanks – I'll take it with me.' He then tipped the contents into a specially prepared pocket and walked away.

Or: there was the eccentric hostess who was giving a garden party. The bread and butter of the sandwiches she offered her guests was real enough, but they were filled with soap.

When Horace Cole died some years ago, a great gap was left in the ranks of ingenious hoaxers. Eventually, it was filled – though not by an individual, but by a television programme called *Candid Camera*.

The idea had been pioneered by the Columbia Broadcasting System in America and was brought to Britain in January 1960. For just over six years it presented some of the most elaborate practical jokes ever played on an unsuspecting public. In all, there were 6,230 of them – most of which were

Interval: A Collection of Hoaxers

thought out by a small team, which included producer Peter Dulay and the man who was, perhaps, Cole's natural successor, a writer and TV performer named Jonathan Routh.

The classic *Candid Camera* joke was probably the one in which Routh arrived at a filling station in a Ford Prefect. He told the attendant to fill it up with petrol, and then tried to start the engine. Nothing happened.

'Would you,' he said to the man, 'look under the bonnet and see if you can find out what's wrong.'

The attendant did as he was asked and saw, to his utter dismay, that there was no engine in the car.

Obviously, a great deal of preparation had gone into the making of the prank. The engine had been removed, and the filling station had been carefully selected. It had to be just around the corner from the bottom of a hill – so that Routh could coast on to the forecourt without arousing any suspicions.

On another occasion, a lady visitor to Blackpool innocently put a coin into a slot machine. Instantly, the machine began to disgorge rivers of pennies. There seemed to be no end to them. The woman tried to catch as many as possible in her skirt, but still they poured forth, spilling over on to the pavement, running on to the road, until there seemed to be pennies everywhere.

The machine had, of course, been modified to such an extent that one of the *Candid Camera* team was concealed behind it, shovelling out the coins.

But this was almost commonplace beside the strange adventure of a girl who applied for a temporary position at an office in London's Baker Street. When she arrived she noticed that, against one of the walls, there was a television set. She was just settling down to work, when an engineer came in and handed her a walky-talky.

'I'm going up on to the roof to adjust the aerial,' he said. 'I shall turn the set on, and I'd be glad if you'd let me know when the picture seems to be most clear.'

The girl agreed: the engineer switched on the box and departed, presumably to carry out his work.

A snooker match was being screened, and the girl watched with rather half-hearted interest until one of the shots showed a ball approaching a pocket. It was almost as if the camera were concealed in the pocket itself, for the ball became bigger and bigger, filling the screen, until – with a crash, it came right through and landed on the thick pile of the office carpet.

Now this was amazing enough. Either TV had taken a dramatic and technically fantastic new turn, or else the poor girl was going out of her mind. But more was to come. Within seconds of the ball crashing through the box, the player who had made the shot poked his head through the hole where the screen had been, and asked: 'Can we have our ball back?'

This was too much. The girl fainted.

Other people on whom the joke was played turned out to be more robust, and it was, in fact, shown in one of the *Candid Camera* programmes. To rig it up, a console model TV set had been gutted, and a piece of rice paper stretched across the opening where the tube had been. A hole was cut in the wall behind it, and a specially made length of film was back-projected on to the rice paper. As the ball appeared in close up, one of the team threw an identical version through the screen. After that, it only remained for the player who had been in the film to stick his head through.

Candid Camera gave a great deal of pleasure to millions of people. Sometimes, it gave just as much to those who were unknowingly taking part in it. One morning, a large supermarket in Twickenham was full of shoppers. Musak was playing soft melodies as Musak in these places is apt to do. And then, suddenly, there was a moment of silence; and then, a man's voice saying: 'Please take your partners for a quickstep.'

Two of the *Candid Camera* team began dancing and,

Interval: A Collection of Hoaxers

before very long, most of the shoppers, their metal baskets hanging from their arms, were joining in. Now and again, it was possible to pick up fragments of conversation – such as, when a woman asked a man: 'Do you come here often?' and the man replied: 'Only on Wednesdays. I'm dancing for the West Country at Tesco's on Thursdays, but they only have tea dances.' The public, it seemed, had gone happily mad and was entering into the spirit of the joke.

Not surprisingly, there were times when *Candid Camera* episodes went wrong. On one occasion, a victim went into a shop and observed that nobody was behind the counter. A man was standing just inside the door, waiting. He said: 'She won't be a minute – she's just gone round the back.'

The man seemed to be taking an intent interest in a tank of goldfish which was decorating one of the walls. That, perhaps, was understandable. What really shook the shopper was when he reached out, grabbed one of the fish, and ate it.

The explanation was simple enough. It was no fish at all, but a carefully carved fragment of carrot. Everything had gone beautifully – with the innocent shopper reacting just as one might have expected him to react. Unfortunately a small boy in Rutland saw the programme and decided that he, too, would like to eat a goldfish. He went next door to a neighbour's house, selected the juiciest specimen in the bowl, and devoured it. The boy suffered no ill effects, but the fish had been a favourite pet of the family's. A great deal of Rutland wrath was heaped on the heads of the *Candid Camera* team.

On two occasions, they had to make rapid departures from the scene of operations. One of them was when they visited a very select corner of North West London. Two of them appeared in the guise of workmen.

It was not long before a busybody came up to ask what they were doing. 'We're supposed to be re-naming your streets, guv'nor,' one of the men said.

'And what are you going to call this one?'

The man produced a sign from his bag. It carried the

words: *Coronation Street*. The resident departed to consult with his neighbours and a crowd began to gather. When somebody else asked what *his* street was to be called, he was shown a board marked *Peyton Place*.

One has to remember that this was a *very* select place: a citadel of the intelligentsia, where nobody would have been seen dead watching *Coronation Street* or *Peyton Place*. Soon the crowd became very angry, and it looked as if a lynching party was preparing to emulate the deeds of the Wild West. The *Candid Camera* men departed in confusion, but content with the thought that they had, at least, obtained some good film from the incident.

But that was one of the days when *nothing* went right. When they tried to play back the sound track, they discovered that the tape-recorder had been incorrectly loaded and had not picked up anything at all.

Another gag involved the use of a telephone kiosk. The idea was that a couple of workmen with pneumatic drills should be stationed outside. An innocent victim was given a message, telling him to call a number immediately. Once through, he would be asked to go to a particular place at a certain time. The moment the conversation arrived at this point – which was, when all is said and done, the most important part – the pneumatic drillers, promptly on cue, would begin to hammer the living daylights out of the street outside. It is as good a way as any of driving unsuspecting people insane.

The first time they tried it was outside a large block of council flats in West London. A friend of one of the housewives was enlisted as an accomplice, and agreed to be beside her telephone at a certain time. Then the victim was given a message, asking her to call her friend urgently.

All went well. The woman went into the phone box: she got through to her friend, who said something to the effect that the two of them should meet at (BANG, BANG, BANG from the drill) on (BANG, BANG, BANG) no – at

Interval: A Collection of Hoaxers

(more BANG, BANG, BANG). No, I *said* BANG, BANG, BANG.

Eventually the woman, halfway out of her mind, retired to the flats. The *Candid Camera* team congratulated themselves that it had gone very well indeed and that, when the victim reappeared, she would be let into their highly amusing little secret.

However, there was murder brewing up in the flats. The woman did come out again, but forty of her friends came with her, and they were undoubtedly out for blood. Not since Boadicea had driven her chariot against the Romans, or the Amazons had terrorized the Greeks, had such a warlike army of women marched into action. By some miracle, doubtless spurred on by the superhuman effort that deadly peril produces, the hoaxers managed to get their compressor, their drills, and themselves safely from the scene before any blood was shed.

Later, they tried the same gag on a taxi driver who, when his ordeal was over, saw the fun of it.

Ideas came from many different sources. Once, the newspapers published the story of a foreign diplomat who had been very nearly smuggled out of Italy in a cabin trunk. This suggested untold possibilities and, before very long, they had a plot worked out.

In the best tradition of the Central Intelligence Agency or the Secret Service, *Candid Camera* had a suite of offices in London which only a very few people knew about. The casual visitor, reading the name plate outside, might have imagined that it was the headquarters of a perfectly normal commercial undertaking. The only thing that might have aroused his suspicion was the fact that the name seemed to change with surprising frequency. *Candid Camera* operated, at any rate from these premises, under whatever pseudonym seemed most appropriate to its jape of the moment.

This time, the offices were to be used for the 'Man in Trunk' mystery. The cameras (always concealed behind a double mirror) were loaded. A volunteer was taking his ease in a trunk on the floor. The team had assembled and were checking up on last minute details. The time was about nine o'clock in the morning. At ten o'clock, the victim – who would be coming from a temporary employment agency, thinking that he was to be offered a short term position as a clerk – would be coming up the three flights of stairs from the street.

'Now don't forget,' Peter Dulay told the man in the trunk, 'when you hear a single tap on the top, you groan. And mind you make it a good groan.'

'Yes, yes,' the man said. 'I'll do that.'

Possibly the victim's watch was fast. At all events, he turned up a good forty-five minutes early. Not that it really mattered – the *Candid Camera* team were pastmasters of improvisation. The cameramen quietly disappeared to their action stations; the lid of the trunk was hurriedly slammed down; and the victim introduced himself.

'What do I have to do?' he asked.

'To begin with,' he was told, 'we'd like you to take this trunk over to the Bulgarian Embassy. Could you do that?'

'Yes,' the man said. And to show his goodwill, he gave the trunk a friendly slap. The man inside got the signal, and let out an entirely convincing and somewhat terrifying groan.

The victim stiffened. 'Funny,' he said. 'I thought I heard ...'

Somebody else slapped the trunk this time, and again the man groaned. The victim was no longer in any doubt. He left the room with the speed of a grand prix racing car, went down the stairs at a great many miles per hour, and ran off down the street with the *Candid Camera* team in pursuit. Eventually, after a desperate chase, they caught up with him before he was able to get hold of a policeman. Although he was very frightened indeed, he accepted their explanation, and the story had a happy ending.

These episodes usually ended that way. Out of all the

Interval: A Collection of Hoaxers

people who were conned by *Candid Camera*, only ten per cent refused to allow the episodes to be screened. To some extent this can be explained by the fact that they were usually prepared to laugh at themselves. Nevertheless, such an attitude was no doubt helped by the fact that, once the truth had been revealed, they were offered payment for their services.

On one occasion, the promise of a reward reacted against the interests of the company responsible for the programme. The scene was a club where the members played bridge. One afternoon, an innocent individual found himself making up a four with (unknown to him) three of the *Candid Camera* boys.

The game was, to say the least, odd. The *Candid Camera* men were making wild calls, passing cards to one another under the table, and generally playing in an entirely eccentric and unseemly manner. At first, the victim was ill at ease. After a bit, he pointed out the irregularities, but was told: 'This is the way we always play it. Do you mind?'

'Well – no,' he said. 'Not if this is the way you wish to play.'

'That's how we wish.'

The game continued.

Some days afterwards, the victim went to see the film with his wife (*Candid Camera* victims were always invited to see clips of the films in which they appeared before giving their consent to the screening of them on TV).

'Do you mind?' he was asked.

'Of course we don't mind,' his wife said. 'After all you'll be paying us. How much?'

They told her what the standard rate was, but the lady protested that it was nothing like enough. Since the film in question was very amusing, the *Candid Camera* men increased the offer. This haggling went on for some days until, at the end, the man received even more than his wife had asked in the first place.

But such snags were rare, and people usually accepted

what they were offered. And, of course, a great many programmes were produced without any snags at all. Two which were outstanding are these:

The scene was a coffee house. A man went in and sat down in an empty seat. Beside the table, there was a bowl with a fine display of tulips. The waitress took his order and presently returned with a cup of tea.

Just as he was about to drink it, one of the tulips leaned over, inserted its head in the cup, and drained the lot.

It was an almost fiendishly clever piece of stage management, with a plastic tube replacing the stem of the flower, linked to a vacuum cleaner, which was concealed in the room next door.

The other episode took place on one of the greens at a golf links. A man had just putted his ball, and was leaning over to take it out of the hole. You can, perhaps, imagine his astonishment, when a hand came out of the ground and gave it back to him.

Here, again, there had been elaborate preparations. Part of the green had been dug up, and a *Candid Camera* crewman buried in such a way that he could get one of his hands into the hole. After that, it was easy.

Although some of the *Candid Camera* incidents were of a sinister, almost frightening, nature (well – wouldn't it worry *you*, seeing a hand coming out of the ground, or a living person poking his head out of your TV set?), the final effect was nearly always comical. Ultimately, the expression on the victim's face mattered just as much as the ingenious ruse which produced it. Indeed, most of the case histories considered in this chapter have been of a frivolous nature. They are not recommended to the serious student of impostors. Nor, indeed, are they recommended to anyone at all, for they might get the hoaxer into real trouble, and there's quite enough of that already.

And now, with the interval over, perhaps we can get back to more serious matters.

6

The Early Morning Men

In the year 1869, two men on a farm near the American village of Cardiff, New York, were busy digging a well. When they were about three feet down, the pickaxe of one of them struck a solid object. He removed the earth from it and saw, to his intense dismay, an enormous toe sticking up.

'What the blazes,' he said to his companion, 'do you figure this is?'

'Looks like a toe,' the man said.

'Sure it's a toe – but did you ever see one this size?'

'Can't say I have,' the man said.

'And it's hard. Hard as a rock. Human toes aren't like that, are they? Your toes aren't that way, surely?'

'Better dig some more,' the man said.

Working more carefully now, the labourer cleared the earth away. Presently a foot was revealed, and then an ankle, and then the lower part of a leg. Each was huge: far, far bigger than any normal man would have had.

'Strikes me,' the second man said, 'we'd better get the boss. This here ain't anyone like you or me.'

The farmer, an individual named Stubby Newell, was away from home. By the time he returned in the afternoon, the two men had dug up a good deal more of the strange creature, and a crowd had gathered around the hole.

'What's happening here?' Newell asked. 'Somebody get hurt?'

'What the blazes,' he said to his companion, *'do you figure this is?'*

'It's those men of yours,' one of the bystanders said. 'Looks like they've dug up a giant.'

And that seemed to be about the strength of it. Lying exposed in a three feet deep grave was the figure of an outsize man who must have been ten feet four inches tall. His body was twisted over to the right and his left foot was turned upwards. Somehow it suggested to everyone present that the unfortunate individual had died in considerable agony.

The labourer who had uncovered the toe came over to Newell. 'What do you think about this?' he asked.

'Seems you've struck giants,' Newell said with a grin.

'Must've been dead a long time,' the man said. 'Ain't any giants, so far as I know, in these parts nowadays.'

The Early Morning Men

'Sure he's been dead a long time. I reckon you've made an important scientific discovery. Could be we're all descended from giants. This guy here could date right back to the early morning of the world.'

'Then how come,' the man said, 'he ain't decomposed? That's what happens to corpses, ain't it? This guy's intact. There's all of him here – why, you can even see the pores in his skin.'

'You never heard of fossils?' Newell said. 'This giant's become fossilized – kind of turned to stone. I did hear they dug up some sort of a fossil in these parts not long ago. But this one here: this one's a really big discovery.'

'You can say it's big all right,' the man said.

The news got around and Cardiff, from being an obscure hamlet which only appeared on a few, large scale, maps, suddenly became important. Tourists came to the village. The local hotel renamed itself 'The Giant Saloon'. Stubby Newell called his home 'Goliath House', and erected a tent over the discovery. Visitors were charged half-a-dollar admission.

It was all excellent for business. Times had been hard in Cardiff, but the attention created by the giant brought good money to the village. Everything was going just fine until the experts came on to the scene.

They asked whether, in view of the light it shed on man's earliest ancestry, they might make a scientific examination of the huge and long lamented individual. Stubby Newell said that they might, though he did not appear to be entirely happy about the idea.

You know how it is with experts: they take a miracle and then use science to show that it has all been done with mirrors. They kill the notion that a strange race of supermen lives on Venus, or that Martians have an elaborate system of canals. Magic walks out the moment an expert comes in.

When they were done with the Cardiff giant, they had exposed – no fresh light on the origins of mankind, no exciting stories of a race of huge men who, over the years, had shrunk – but an ingenious plot.

The giant had nothing to do with flesh and blood and bones. The experts discovered that he had been carved out of a five-ton block of gypsum. A great deal of trouble had been taken to make him appear real. The pores in the skin, for instance, had been created by hammering lead needles into the rock. In other words, he was a sham, a complete impostor. He was a fine work of art no doubt, but his scientific value was nil.*

A cigar manufacturer named George Hull was the man behind the hoax, which had been carried out with the cooperation of Stubby Newell. The 'giant' had been brought to the farm on a wagon at dead of night, and buried. Newell's idea of digging a new well had only been a means of ensuring that it was discovered. While the deception lasted, it brought prosperity to Cardiff, NY. But, as they say, you can't beat the experts.

Experts never give up. For so long as there is any doubt at all about anything, they delve away – searching for the truth. It may take them four hours, or it may take them forty years, but they get there in the end. Perhaps it is just as well, though it spoils some very good stories.

Take, for example, the case of the Piltdown man. Piltdown is a small village in Sussex, not far from the town of Uckfield. In 1890, a solicitor named Charles Dawson moved from London to Uckfield. He became clerk to the local magistrates and also looked after the affairs of several large estates in the vicinity. Among them was Barkham Manor at Piltdown.

* According to the Guinness Book of Records, the tallest man ever was Robert Pershing Wadlow, who lived from 1918 until 1940 and was 8 feet 11.09 inches high. In Britain, Henry Blacker was born in 1724 near the Sussex village of Cuckfield. When he grew up, he reached the height of 7 feet 4 inches.

The Early Morning Men

Charles Dawson was an able lawyer, but he had other skills. He was a Fellow of the Society of Antiquaries and also a competent amateur geologist. He discovered a deposit of natural gas near the village of Heathfield and, for a good many years, it was used in the lamps at the local railway station.

One day, according to his version of the story, he had been walking in the grounds of Barkham Manor, when he came upon some men carrying out repairs to a farm road. His geologist's eye noticed that the flints they were using were not common to the district, and this aroused his curiosity. The men told him that they had been dug up at a nearby farm. He asked them whether they had discovered any bones or fossils there. They said that they had not.

A few years went by, and then Dawson suddenly sprung a remarkable discovery on the scientific world. He had, he told a gathering of experts in 1912, found fresh evidence on the origins of man. Digging away at the farm where the flints had come from, he had unearthed fragments of a human skull's brain case, a jaw bone with teeth in it, and some flint implements. Put together, they suggested that human beings had been living in the region half a million years ago. This would have been during the early Ice Age, and it was fair to assume, he said, that, among the animals of that period, there would have been hippopotamus, elephant, deer, beavers and horses. Later, as if to confirm his theory, he unearthed a crude implement in the shape of a club, which had been fashioned out of an elephant's bone. Some while later, he made some more, similar, discoveries at a site about two miles away in Sheffield Park.

But, by then, World War I had broken out. Charles Dawson had been busy inventing 'flaming bullets' with which to shoot down enemy airships (they were never used) and he was a sick man. He died on August 10th, 1916.

During his final illness and for some time after his death, a good deal of work was done in the region of Piltdown and

Sheffield Park, searching for more evidence. But nothing more came to light. The Piltdown man must, it seemed, have been a loner.

Soon after he had announced his discovery, Dawson handed over the fragments of the skull, the jaw and the teeth to the British Museum. They had turned brown with age – as might have been expected. But there were several mysterious things about them. For example, if it had not been for the teeth, the jaw might have been mistaken for that of a chimpanzee. Their surfaces, however, had been flattened by wear in a way that is characteristic of a man but not of an ape.

The fragments of the brain case, on the other hand, were quite clearly those of a human being, and of a comparatively intelligent one at that. This was odd. All the evidence before and after the discovery of the Piltdown man suggested that man's jaw achieved its present shape fairly early on in the process of evolution. It was the brain which had taken such a long time to develop.

Had it not been for the teeth, it might have been reasonable to assume that these were the remains of two creatures, both belonging to the same period: a man and a chimpanzee. In the very early Ice Age, that might have been possible. Later on, it would not have been. By the late Ice Age (about 50,000 years ago) there were no longer any apes in Britain – nor, indeed, anywhere else in Europe.

Clearly, the Piltdown man was a very interesting character. As the missing link between men and monkeys, he stubbornly refused to fit in with all the findings from other parts of the world. He had, for no other conclusion was possible, to be the odd man out.

The years went by. No more discoveries were made. There was still a question mark hanging over this remarkable individual, but nothing shed any fresh light on it.

After the last war, the subject cropped up again. By this time, more sophisticated methods were available for study-

The Early Morning Men

ing the evidence. One of them was the fluoroscope: another was the geiger counter.

Fluorine is a substance which is present in damp soil. It builds up deposits in buried bones and teeth, and a fluoroscope is used to determine how much is present. Provided they have been discovered fairly close together, it can tell the researcher whether a collection of bones are all of the same age, or whether they belong to different periods of prehistory.

In 1949, a fluoroscope was applied to the skull and the jawbone of the Piltdown man. The results were surprising and instantly demolished the idea of a reasonably intelligent human being, with the jaw of an ape, good with his hands and capable of making rudimentary tools, stalking the Sussex countryside 500,000 years ago. For the better part of forty years, he had been a kind of chinless wonder, causing endless dispute and, as it turned out, making a mockery of the men who tried to discover his real identity.

Now, the truth was to be known.

The first tests by the fluoroscope showed that he was nothing like so old as the experts had expected. These experiments suggested that the jaw and the skull were, indeed, of the same period, but that they were no more than 50,000 years old – when the large skull might have been expected, but the chinless jaw was still something of a poser. Elsewhere in the world, men had developed their modern jaws long before that.

A year or two later, however, more tests were carried out. This time, they revealed that, although the skull was certainly 50,000 (give or take a century) years old, the jaw was nothing like so antique. Experiments with a geiger counter, used to measure the amount of radioactivity present, confirmed this fact. It had, whatever the evidence of the teeth suggested, to belong to a relatively modern ape.

But were the teeth really so important? One fact about them had been puzzling the experts for some time.

Obviously nobody could tell for how long they had been munching away at whatever this primitive man ate; but, even so, they seemed to be more worn than their active life suggested. Was there something phoney about them?

A scientist took an ape's tooth and carefully filed down the front and back. The effect was very much like that of the Piltdown man's. Further tests showed that this was exactly what had been done; and that, furthermore, the skull and the jaw bone had been artfully coloured in such a way that they *seemed* to be of the same age.

Suspicion now fell on the flint instruments and the clublike tool which had been fashioned from the bone of an elephant. A minute examination suggested that the latter had been worked on by somebody using a steel blade, and there were certainly none of those in circulation 50,000 years ago – let alone half a million years ago. As for the flint implements, an exhaustive search revealed that they could not possibly have come from Sussex. Their probable place of origin was somewhere near the town of Bizerta in Tunisia.

So: what did it all add up to? The Piltdown man was an impostor. A cleverly conceived and brilliantly executed hoax which had fooled the greatest scientific brains for nearly half a century. It was only with the coming of modern research methods that their real nature was exposed. Somehow, by somebody, they had been planted.

The ape's jaw and the flints and the elephant bone – none of these would have been difficult to obtain. At the beginning of this century there were a number of shops at which anyone could have bought them. The skull, perhaps, was more of a problem. But, in 1954, a lady living in Sussex recalled how, in 1906, her father had given Charles Dawson an unusual human skull. It was brown with age, had no lower jaw bone, and there was a mark, rather as if it had received a blow of some sort, on the forehead. Apparently, Dawson had said: 'You'll hear more about this.' This, possibly, fills in the missing part.

But, if it does, we have to conclude that Charles Dawson created the impostor: that he was a hoaxer of considerable magnitude, a planter of false evidence, an archaeological forger. Can this really be true?

He was a learned and much respected man. He had a position in the neighbourhood and was a prominent member of the Hastings Natural History Society. In these circles, however, he did not enjoy the esteem which came to him with the discovery of the Piltdown man. A *History of Hastings Castle* written by him (it was a heavyweight work in two volumes) received a good deal of criticism, and the locals seem to have found him 'proud and ambitious', and not entirely to their liking.

But none of this suggests that he was in any way dishonest. According to the law, a man must be considered innocent unless it has been proven, *beyond any reasonable doubt*, that he is guilty. If this criterion were applied to Charles Dawson, he certainly could not be convicted of the Piltdown forgery. But if the onus were on Dawson to prove his innocence, he would have had a very difficult task. Of all the people concerned in the Piltdown affair, he was the only one to be in possession of all the facts, and it must be remembered that, when he succumbed to the illness which caused his death, the supply of evidence dried up at once.

Everything pointed to Dawson unless some other person were involved: somebody, that is to say, who has never been suspected. This mystery man might have used the Sussex solicitor as his tool – as a means of discovering the evidence which set the world talking. Or, he might have hoped that the fraud would have been discovered during Dawson's lifetime so that the latter would have been discredited and disgraced. His motive, in such a case, might have been to pay off a grudge.

But this is somewhat far-fetched. It is much easier to find motives to suggest that Dawson perpetrated the fraud. If he did so, and if it had been in the hope of winning fame, he certainly succeeded. The brain case and the jaw bone were named *Eoanthropus dawsoni* in honour of the man who found them. And, as late as 1938, a memorial stone was unveiled to his memory at the gravel pit where they had been discovered. It was not until a full forty years after the advent of the Piltdown man that the words *Eoanthropus dawsoni* were uttered with anything short of reverence.

An alternative idea, of course, is that Dawson may have been a practical joker: that the hoax, as these things sometimes do, went too far and that, having awakened the interest and respect of the scientific world, he had to maintain it. If this is so, and it seems to be the most charitable solution from Dawson's point of view, it wasted an enormous amount of time and filled hundreds of learned pages to very little purpose.

A reconstruction of the Piltdown skull suggests that, like all skulls, it is grinning at us. But in this case, perhaps, it is not just an impression. If there is laughter in its two rows of smirking teeth, there is plenty of reason for it. The Piltdown man, Dawson or no Dawson, fooled the experts for several decades. But, as usually happens, they got him in the end.

The General

'By God,' the General said to himself, 'I feel ill.' He looked at his face in the mirror, and decided it did not belong to a fit man. The words of his medical officer came back to him. 'You really ought to take things more easily,' he had said. More easily! How could a man in his position do that?

As Commander-in-Chief of the German 7th Army, his responsibilities were enormous. It was something they never seemed to appreciate back in Berlin. Whenever visitors came to see him from the capital, they seldom strayed far from headquarters in Le Mans. It was fine from their point of view: a pleasant French town, a good lunch at the leading hotel, some routine chatter, and off they went.

They probably thought it was fine for him, too: a comfortable headquarters in a lovely old château, quiet countryside outside, and neat files of trees on either side of the drive – what more could a man want? Perhaps he was lucky, but the thought was no great consolation to him.

He sat down at his desk and swallowed a couple of pills. They made him feel slightly better. 'Couldn't you manage to take some leave?' the medical officer had asked.

How could a man go on leave at a time like this? It was May 1944, and things were not going at all well for the German armed forces. There had been heavy reversals in Russia. They'd been kicked out of North Africa over a year ago, and now the British and the Americans were creeping up Italy like the leading edge of a forest fire.

And things were going to become worse. The General had no doubt about this. All the Intelligence reports suggested that an invasion of France was imminent. France! By heaven, if they came through Normandy, it would not be long before his own troops were involved.

He sighed. The pills took away the pain, but he still felt tired. 'I ought to be in bed,' he told himself.

There was a knock on his door.

'Yes?' he said wearily.

His *aide de camp* came in. 'Telegram for you, sir,' he said.

'Read it to me,' the General said. 'Who's it from?'

'General von Blaskowitz, Berlin. He's on his way here – wants to see round some of the defences. According to this, he should be arriving very shortly.'

The General put his head in his hands, leaning heavily on his elbows. 'As if life were not complicated enough,' he muttered.

'Sir?'

'Never mind. Let me know the moment he arrives. And you'd better get somebody to arrange lunch at the Hotel de Paris.'

'Yes, sir. Forgive me ...'

'What is it?'

'The General does not look at all well.'

'The General feels damned ill, but never mind. We must see that this Blaskowitz has every facility. We don't want him taking back an adverse report to Hitler, do we?'

'No, sir. Indeed we don't.'

The *aide de camp* saluted and walked out of the room.

'At least he doesn't give me that "Heil Hitler" nonsense,' the General thought. He turned unhappily to the pile of papers on his desk.

About an hour later, there was a great deal of noise outside. It sounded as if an entire armoured corps had drawn up, but a quick glance from the window showed that it was only a

The General

staff car. The din was mostly made by the guards, who were coming to attention with such alacrity that they seemed to be trying to stamp holes in the earth's crust.

'General Blaskowitz has arrived,' his *aide de camp* said from the doorway.

'Thank you,' said the general and went out to meet his guest.

'Good to have you here, General. It's the first time we've enjoyed a visit from you.'

'And pleasant to be here, my dear General Dellmann,' Blaskowitz said. 'It is always good to get away from Berlin. Things there are rather tense, as you may suspect.'

'Yes – I had imagined. Will you be staying the night here?'

'Unfortunately – no.' Blaskowitz turned the corners of his mouth down in a mock frown. 'I have to get back as soon as possible. Sometimes I feel that my presence is necessary to keep the war going.'

'Then let me invite you to take a little refreshment. You must feel like something after your long journey.'

'Thank you – no,' Blaskowitz said. 'I have much to see. Afterwards, perhaps – a little lunch.'

'I quite understand. You must tell me what you'd like to look at.'

They must have travelled the better part of one hundred miles. General Blaskowitz insisted on seeing everything. They toured block houses, and underground bunkers, studied tank traps and barbed wire entanglements, inspected gun positions, viewed the communications systems with, all the while, Blaskowitz asking question after question.

Towards the end of the journey, as they were headed towards the Hotel de Paris in the centre of Le Mans, Blaskowitz said: 'A fine set-up you have here, Dellmann. I cannot imagine how much the French underground movement would like to see what I have seen this morning.'

General Blaskowitz insisted in seeing everything, asking question after question

The General

General Dellmann winced, and felt another of those warning pains from the direction of his heart. 'Please don't mention them,' he said. 'They are a constant worry to me. You cannot imagine how fortunate you are in Germany. At least you are among your own people. They can be trusted. Here we can trust nobody.'

'No,' said Blaskowitz. And then suddenly he laughed – as if he had found his companion's remark amusing.

'Did I say something funny?' Dellmann asked.

'No – no, I assure you. I was merely thinking that at least you don't have the air raids to contend with. I cannot think why I laughed.'

'And how,' Dellmann asked, only too pleased to change the subject, 'is the dear Führer? Well – I trust?'

'Hitler has never been better. A little short-tempered sometimes, but that is only to be expected. My goodness, but I'm hungry.'

'I think you will find the Paris very good. They even keep a supply of schnapps especially for my guests.'

'How good it is that, even in France, one can find a corner of the Fatherland.'

General Blaskowitz, as became his high position, was entertained lavishly. Afterwards, they drove back to the 7th Army headquarters, where he picked up his staff car and driver. Amid a great deal of heel-clicking, he was seen safely off the premises. General Dellmann retired to his office, took two more pills, and lay down on the settee.

He was beginning to doze off, when the door opened and his *aide de camp* came in. The poor fellow looked nervous.

'What is it?' Dellmann asked.

'Another telegram from Berlin,' the *aide de camp* said. 'It could be bad news.'

'I don't think I understand.'

'It's about General Blaskowitz.'

'Well – what about him?'

'This telegram says that he will not be coming, sir. That the visit has been called off.'

Dellmann sat up with a start. 'Not coming?' he exclaimed. 'But he's just been here. You saw him for yourself. There must be a mistake. Ring up Berlin and find out what the devil they're playing at.'

'We've already done that, sir,' the *aide de camp* said. 'There is no mistake. Indeed, I have spoken to the General. He is in his room at headquarters. The man who has just been here was not General Blaskowitz.'

'Oh my God,' the General sighed. 'What can have gone wrong? Who *was* he? Tell the Chief of Staff to come here at once. That man must be caught at all costs. Do you realize that he has seen all our secret defences? If he was a member of the French resistance ...'

The General pressed his hand against his chest. 'Could you pass me those tablets ... those pink ones. Thank you.' He took one and the violent pains eased off. 'The Chief of Staff, please. The man must be found at once.'

They never found the bogus General Blaskowitz. His staff car was discovered abandoned some miles down the road which leads from Le Mans to Paris. It turned out to have been stolen from one of the Army's transport pools. General Dellmann's visitor and his driver were, as he had feared, both members of the French underground movement. They had acquired their uniforms a few days earlier in Paris. How they discovered about Blaskowitz's proposed visit, and how that visit came to be cancelled, are mysteries which have never been solved. What is for certain is that, on that same day, the Allied headquarters in Britain were given full details of the German 7th Army's defensive positions. It was knowledge which turned out to be extremely useful during the fighting which followed 'D' Day. But General Dellmann knew nothing about that. A few days before the Allied invasion, he died of a heart attack.

8

All Is not Gold

People will believe whatever they *want* to believe. No matter how silly it is, nor how wrong the facts, if they are really anxious for something to be true, then they'll insist that it *is* true.

Take the case of gold. It is a metallic element which is mined. It is proof against most acids, and is quite a pleasant substance from which to manufacture jewellery. Otherwise, it is useless. You cannot make ball bearings out of it, or ships, or houses, or motor cars, or television sets, or anything else which is useful to mankind. And yet, for some extraordinary reason, it is valued above all others. It is, and always has been, the very symbol of wealth.

People go mad about gold. They will do anything, go anywhere, and sometimes believe anything – if they imagine that it will provide them with a helping of this precious substance. Sometimes they will also make complete fools of themselves.

The private sitting-room in Munich's most expensive hotel was crowded that evening. They were all well-to-do people: the men were wearing dinner jackets and the women were clad in fashionable evening dresses. At first glance, it might have seemed to be an important social function. Everybody was holding a glass of champagne, and the men were smoking big cigars. The only thing that appeared to be wrong, was that hardly anyone was talking. Indeed, if one looked at them carefully, one came to the conclusion that they seemed to be rather suspicious of one another.

At the far end of the room, there was a small table. A steel plate, a common-or-garden salt cellar, and a lamp with a large green shade were laid out upon it. Beside it, a small man with an alert face and a pair of wire-rimmed spectacles was thoughtfully studying a handful of notes. Presently he rapped on the table.

'Ladies and gentlemen,' he said. 'If you would care to sit down, I will tell you why we are all gathered here.'

Some of the women seated themselves: most of the men remained standing. A number of them edged closer to the table.

'My name is Hans Unruh,' the little man said, 'and I must ask you to treat what I am about to tell you with the strictest confidence. I really mean that,' and he smiled. 'This is not a secret to be shared, but one to keep strictly to yourselves. It is very, very important, and it could be dangerous.'

He paused dramatically. One or two of the men made 'pooh, pooh!' noises, as if they were accustomed to rubbing shoulders with danger every day of the week. The women leaned hopefully forward. This, they told themselves, was going to be good.

'Ladies and gentlemen,' Herr Unruh said, 'I am about to demonstrate to you the most important discovery of the century. Indeed, I will go further. It may very well be the greatest thing that has ever been discovered in the history of the world. Only one thing could be more so, and that would be the secret of everlasting life.' Another quick smile. 'But I am afraid I have no news for you about that.'

He looked down at the items on the table and carefully picked up the salt cellar. 'I want you to look at this closely,' he said. 'This contains ordinary table salt. I am not deluding you. You can, if you wish, taste a sample of it. Would anyone care to?'

All Is not Gold

Nobody cared to. One of the men said: 'Go on, Herr Unruh – we'll believe you.'

'Very well,' the little man continued. 'This is what I have to tell you. We call it "common" salt, but it is not so common as that. Chemists have no doubt learned a good deal about it; but, believe me, they have not learned enough. As I shall show you in a moment or two, this may very well be one of the most precious commodities on earth.'

'But that's nonsense,' a woman with a rather shrill voice interrupted him. 'Salt is just – well, salt. Everybody knows that.'

'If you will bear with me, madam,' Herr Unruh said politely, 'I shall hope to show you that this is not so. Salt, and this is something which has never been known before, is the substance of *gold*.'

Another dramatic pause. Somebody exclaimed: 'Oh I say – that's a bit far-fetched,' and another grunted: 'Rubbish!'

'No, sir,' Herr Unruh said. 'Not "rubbish". Be patient – you will see. I am a scientist, and I have been fortunate enough to discover the very nature of gold. Have you ever considered how it is produced? I will tell you.

'It comes from the depths of the earth, and it is caused by a certain chemical action which takes place on what we have dismissed as unimportant salt. If some method could be discovered of reproducing this chemical change, gold could be manufactured. Think of it, ladies and gentlemen – a grain of gold dust for every crystal of salt. The wealth of it is beyond imagining.'

'But how could that ever happen?' one of the men asked.

'By a piece of apparatus I have here.' Herr Unruh pointed to the green lampshade. 'After a great deal of very painstaking research, I have discovered the secret. I have found that, if you treat the salt with a special form of light, it will turn into gold. No, ladies and gentlemen – I am not describing a miracle. I am talking about a straightforward scientific fact. The effect of this light, very simply, is to reproduce the chemical process which takes place deep down inside the earth.

'Now – I beg you, watch very carefully.'

Taking up the salt cellar once more, he gently scattered the contents on to the steel plate. He then took the lamp and held it in such a position that the shade completely covered the dish. He switched the lamp on.

'We must wait for a few moments while the change is taking place,' he said. 'I am sorry that I cannot allow the waiters in to refill your glasses, but I am sure that you must be beginning to see how important this is. There are many people who would sell their souls to possess my secret. I dare not risk such an occurrence. And do not be alarmed, ladies and gentlemen. I shall not be asking for your souls at the end of this meeting.' He laughed, and there were one or two titters from his guests. 'You are here to listen to a straightforward business proposition. Nothing more.'

He tapped the lampshade, and then smiled at his audience. 'Well,' he said. 'I think that's done. Now – watch.'

As Herr Unruh slowly took the lamp away from the plate, there was a profound silence in the room. Nobody spoke. Nobody moved. They sat there and they stood there, and they were all staring at the steel plate.

Presto! Herr Unruh had been as good as his word. The salt was all gone. In its place, there was a substantial pile of gold dust.

'Great heavens!' one of the men said.

And: 'It's really true,' from a woman.

'Yes, madam – it's quite true,' Herr Unruh said. 'Now you can see for yourselves.' He held up the plate and the gold shone and the faces of the audience seemed to be transformed into a mixture of ecstasy and greed.

'With your permission,' Herr Unruh said, 'I shall now put this safely into a bag. It is not, you must agree, something which can be left lying about.' He extracted a small canvas sack from his pocket and tipped the gold dust neatly inside

All Is not Gold

it. When he had done, he said: 'Now, perhaps, you have some questions?'

'I have one,' a man said. 'This was a remarkable display, and I can see why it will benefit you, but how can it help us? Why have you invited us here to see it?'

'Quite simple,' Herr Unruh smiled. 'Believe me, ladies and gentlemen, I have not been wasting your valuable time. I think I may have convinced you that I know how to manufacture gold. But, as you can see, I can only do so in small quantities. To make it worth while, a much larger piece of apparatus is needed. Now that I have discovered the method, this would not be difficult to manufacture, but it requires capital. I am not a wealthy man. Just a poor, struggling, scientist, you might say; and that is why you are here. I wish to invite you all to become shareholders in my enterprise. You have all of you been specially selected for this opportunity. You are wealthy, of proven integrity and with a great sense of responsibility. These things I know. It is only to such people as your good selves, that I would dare to entrust my secret. Perhaps you would like to go away now and think it over. If anyone cares to take advantage of my offer, I shall still be here in the morning.'

'The others can please themselves,' one of the men said, 'but I want to do something about it now. How much are your shares?'

An epidemic of gold fever had begun. By the time Herr Unruh's guests dispersed, nearly all of them had bought shares in his enterprise.

About a week later, a similar meeting took place at a luxury apartment in Berlin. When it was over, Herr Unruh poured himself a glass of wine and lit a cigarette.

'Do you know,' he told his wife – who had been sitting in a corner of the large sofa, 'I feel tired.'

'I'm not surprised. Was it a good evening?'

'Remarkably. I think we've made about £5,300. Of course

the cheque from that Prussian merchant helped. He subscribed £2,600.'

'It was good,' his wife agreed. 'Where are you going to put on the next show?'

'No more shows,' Herr Unruh said. 'We'll have to think of something else. I really cannot believe that we'd get away with it a third time. When you come to think of it, it isn't even a very good conjuring trick. If I did it in front of an audience of children, they'd see how it was done in no time at all.'

'They wouldn't be thinking so much about the gold,' his wife said.

'Yes – I suppose that is apt to cloud people's judgement.'

The trick was simple. The 'gold' was concealed in the green lampshade. When Herr Unruh tapped it, it became dislodged, fell down, and covered the salt. That was why he was so anxious to put it safely away in his little canvas sack. As a matter of fact, it was not gold at all. Just little specks of brass.

People have hungered after gold, and people have even died for it – which seems a remarkably stupid thing to do. When Walter Edward Scott came to Los Angeles in 1905, he appeared, to those who understood these things, to smell of the stuff. For one thing, whenever he bought a drink in a bar, he paid for it with a 500-dollar bill. For another, he made several cryptic references to a 'find up in Death Valley'.

United States citizens do not proffer 500-dollar bills for drinks unless they are remarkably well heeled, and Walter Edward Scott appeared to be literally in this enviable condition. He had so much money in his pockets, that, when he was given change, he was apt to stuff the currency into his boots.

Los Angeles may be Spanish for 'the angels', but whatever cherubims and seraphims may have inhabited the place departed a long, long time ago. Many of the hangers-on who

All Is not Gold

were attracted by Walter Edward Scott's all too apparent wealth were exceedingly non-angelic. Some of them, indeed, even went so far as to pick his pockets. After a while, he grew tired of the attempts by their greedy little hands to lighten his substantial load, and he decided to teach them a lesson.

For a short while, he kept his currency confined to the pockets inside his jacket, and stuffed the outside ones with fish hooks. Up to a point, it was a good idea, and a number of furtive fingers retired from the hunt with severe cuts and scratches. Unfortunately Walter Edward Scott was a somewhat absent-minded character. When reaching for a cigar, or a match, or even for money, he was apt to forget about his booby trap. Consequently, for every scratch on a felon's finger, there were at least two on his own. In the end, he got fed up with fish hooks, threw them away, and resolved to be more careful.

You had to hand it to him, though. He was obviously fabulously rich, and it did not require very much imagination to realize that he probably *had* struck gold up in Death Valley. But there was nothing mean about him. When you were in his company, it was he who did the entertaining, and very nice it was, too.

He also thought *big* – had, you might say, the most original ideas. On one occasion, he decided he'd like to make a trip to Chicago by train. It is a pretty fair distance from Los Angeles to Chicago, and when he challenged the railway company to do the journey in forty-five hours, they told him that he was obviously joking. But Walter Edward Scott was not – and, just to prove it, he offered the company one hundred dollars for every minute they could do it in less than that time.

No self-respecting railway company could ignore such a challenge, especially when it could be turned to very good purpose from a publicity point of view. They assembled a special train, called it 'The Death Valley Special' and, after obtaining their client's permission, invited a party of newspaper men to go along for the ride. Champagne was served in the dining car, Walter Edward Scott was on the top of his glad-handing form, and it looked like being a very agreeable outing.

The train was romping along like a racing car when, at the approaches to Kansas City station, it jumped the tracks. The erstwhile angels of Los Angeles were clearly on the side of the railway company that day. What should have been a major disaster caused relatively little damage. With quite remarkable alacrity, the coaches were hoisted back on to the tracks by crane, and, with a plume of smoke streaming bravely away from its chimney, the locomotive hurried on towards the north. When they reached Chicago, it was discovered that, in spite of the mishap, they were six minutes early. Walter Edward Scott handed over 600 dollars with a smile of congratulations, and the railway company rejoiced in a record that remained unbroken for the next thirty years.

On his return to Los Angeles, Scott spent another day or so enjoying himself, and then muttered something about 'Well – I'd better be getting back.' During the following months, he made several trips to town. They were mostly brief and always ended with his mounting his horse and riding away to the shack he occupied 200 miles away in Death Valley.

Some of the more astute citizens assumed that where Walter Edward Scott's home was, there, too, was a gold mine. They also deduced that where one man has struck gold, others may equally well find it. This gave them the idea of trying to follow Scott. Not obviously, you understand, but – well, shadowing him.

This, as it turned out, was not a very prudent thing to do. Death Valley is rightly named, and to become lost in it is no plight for anyone who gives so much as a cent for his life. Scott was a wily old wizard, and he always seemed to know

All Is not Gold

when a gold hungry character was following in the hoof marks of his horse. He clearly knew the country backwards, which was more than they did. Without, apparently, any difficulty at all, he shook them off and left them to find their own ways home. Many returned to Los Angeles considerably the worse for wear, burned almost black by the desert sun and afflicted with a most fearful thirst. Some never returned at all.

Perhaps it seemed strange that a man who had so much money should continue to live in a humble shack. Most millionaires built palaces for themselves, bought steam yachts, and were driven by chauffeurs in expensive motor cars. But then, people said, everybody was entitled to his eccentricities – especially when he had as many 500-dollar bills in his pockets as Scott had.

But there then occurred the most strange thing of all. It was suddenly discovered that, all this while, the builders had been busy in Death Valley. Next to Scott's old shack, they had erected a fabulous Moorish castle – the kind of place that even a Sultan would be proud to occupy and which had, at a conservative estimate, cost the better part of two million dollars.

Suddenly the way to Death Valley and the Scott property was opened up. Parties of tourists were invited to visit the castle, which became a big attraction. When they arrived there, they saw no gold mines in the vicinity, but there, nestling coyly in the shade of the great building, was Walter Edward Scott's little old shack. And, which is more, he was still living there.

'Truly,' they said as they looked at it, 'this remarkable man's eccentricity knows no limits.'

As they disembarked from their coach, they were even more surprised. Instead of the powdered flunkeys, the army of guides, the retinue of slaves, which they had expected, there was only the old gold miner himself.

'Ladies and gentlemen,' he would say, 'welcome to Death

Valley. It will now give me great pleasure to take you round this great Moorish castle which has been erected at a cost of over two million dollars. As you will see, no expense has been spared to re-create the type of exotic building in which the rulers of Morocco live. And now, if you will kindly follow me ...'

A fabulous Moorish castle had been erected

They all agreed that he was a most efficient guide: rather different, perhaps, from the flamboyant Walter Edward Scott who was so popular in the bars of Los Angeles, but good with the patter and full of information. At times, you almost forgot how rich he was, and that this was *his* castle. Indeed, some visitors found that, had they not thought better of it just in time, they might have given him a dollar tip.

Gold? There was none in Death Valley. Walter Edward Scott? Just a nice, rather amusing, character who was being paid to do a job of work. The truth was a long time in coming out, and it was not until 1941 that the facts became

All Is not Gold

known. The whole thing was a most elaborate hoax, financed by a real millionaire named Albert M. Johnson. Like all other exceptionally rich people, Johnson was an unwilling prey of the tax collector. By financing an operation which was all loss and no profit whatsoever, he paid rather less surtax. And, which pleased him considerably, it gave him a lot to laugh about.

9

The Life and Death of Major Martin

Major William Martin of the Royal Marines sleeps soundly. One day towards the end of April 1943, he was buried near the Spanish town of Huelva. He had been killed in an air crash while on his way to North Africa. Back in Britain, his fiancée – a pleasant girl named Pam – mourned her departed lover. His rather old-fashioned father gazed sadly from the window of an hotel in North Wales, and contemplated the impossibility of wartime romances. The joint general manager of Lloyds Bank spared a thought for an overdraft of £79.98, which might never be repaid. Major Martin's name appeared in the newspaper casualty lists; the Naval and Military Club struck him off its roll of members; and a firm of solicitors arranged to pay a legacy of £50 to the dead officer's servant.

He was, you must agree, a very real person. And yet the remarkable thing about Major William Martin is that he never existed. Along with 'Pam', his 'father', and everything else about him, he was just a figment of the imagination.

Guns are not the only weapons in warfare. Just as a boxer sometimes feints to mislead his opponent, so do hostile nations employ ruses in attempts to deceive one another. After the Germans had been beaten in North Africa, the next target for the British and American forces was Sicily. Once that island had been conquered, the Allies would be able to invade Italy. This was the plan. According to

The Life and Death of Major Martin

Winston Churchill, 'anybody but a damn' fool' would have known what the next objective had to be, and the enemy were certainly not fools. The danger was that they might anticipate the Allied strategy: bring heavy reinforcements to the island, and so create substantial casualties and make the task very much harder.

How admirable it would be if they could be hoaxed! Suppose they could be supplied with 'secret' documents which caused them to think that any operations against Sicily were only a diversion. Suppose they were persuaded to believe Greece and Sardinia were about to be invaded, and that their existing forces in Sicily could be left to take care of themselves. The whole operation would be very much easier and countless lives might be saved.

Compiling documents to create such an impression would not be difficult, but how could they reach the German high command without arousing suspicions? If they were to be believed, the method had to be completely convincing. After all, if the enemy intelligence officers got hold of them too easily, they would sense that the whole thing was a plot. They would forget all about Greece and Sardinia, and strengthen the fortifications in the area about to be attacked.

The answer to this problem was conceived in a highly secret department of the Admirality, and was given the code name of 'Operation Mincemeat'. It was a brilliantly clever idea, which depended – in theory, at any rate – on breaking one unbreakable rule. There were strict instructions that, whenever Allied Officers travelled in aircraft, they must never carry secret documents with them. The reason was obvious. If the aeroplane crashed, the papers might fall into hostile hands.

For the purposes of 'Operation Mincemeat', this regulation had to be overlooked. An aircraft, let us say, was *en route* to Allied headquarters in North Africa. Among those on board was an officer carrying secret papers. Somewhere on the way, the aeroplane crashed, and he was killed. His body was washed ashore, and his briefcase came into the possession of an enemy agent.

It was logical enough and, provided it was carefully executed, it need not arouse any doubts about the genuineness of the documents. If the body was discovered off the coast of Spain, there was a very sporting chance that the material would be transmitted to German Intelligence. The country, admittedly, was neutral, but the Government had fairly strong German sympathies. The place was full of German agents, and a briefcase which was attached to the body of a dead British officer was bound to arouse their interest.

Nor was there any need for an actual air disaster to take place. When an aeroplane crashes into the sea, it is nearly always lost without trace. Little is left floating on the surface, and nothing is washed ashore. All that was needed for an operation that might save thousands of lives was one dead body.

The men planning the deception sought the advice of the hydrographer at the Admiralty. This learned gentleman had an unrivalled knowledge of winds and tides. He was able to tell them that, if the body was put into the sea from a submarine at a certain time on a particular night and at a carefully calculated position on the chart, it would drift ashore at a point somewhere near Huelva on the south coast of Spain.

It was now a question of finding a suitable body. The man had to be in his early thirties, and had to appear to have been the victim of an air crash at sea. The Spanish authorities would almost certainly submit the corpse to a post mortem. If their suspicions were aroused, the fake papers would be discredited.

Eventually they obtained the body of a young man of the right age, who had recently died of pneumonia following a period of exposure. Sir Bernard Spilsbury, the famous Home Office pathologist who had helped to solve several notorious murder cases, said that it would deceive the Spaniards. The

The Life and Death of Major Martin 107

dead man's family agreed to its being used – providing it eventually received a proper burial, and that the identity of the corpse was never published.

So far, so good. The planners had found that their idea was possible, and they had also managed to discover a suitable 'courier' to carry the vital documents. But this was only a beginning. They had to obtain the permission of the chiefs of staff to carry out their scheme; they had to collect suitably worded documents to deceive the enemy; and they had to create a human being. Somehow, the grim messenger had to be given an identity.

After a good deal of discussion, the chiefs of staff gave their consent to 'Operation Mincemeat'. General Sir Archibald Nye, who was Vice-Chief of the Imperial General Staff, agreed to write a letter to General Alexander, who commanded the 18th Army in North Africa. Admiral Lord Louis Mountbatten (now Admiral of the Fleet Earl Mountbatten of Burma) undertook to provide letters addressed to the Commander-in-Chief Mediterranean, and also to General Eisenhower, who was the supreme commander in North Africa.

These documents were of the greatest importance. Obviously, they had to seem to be worth entrusting to a special courier, instead of being sent by the usual route. Furthermore, they had to contain the false information which would mislead the Germans, and cause them to change their ideas about Sicily as the target for an Allied invasion.

Both men did their work admirably. In his letter to General Alexander, Sir Archibald Nye referred to a planned assault by one division, reinforced by a brigade, on Cape Araxos in Greece. He talked about Sicily as a 'cover' for this operation, and he included the kind of military chat that is to be expected when one general writes to another.

Lord Mountbatten introduced the bearer of his letter to the Commander-in-Chief as a member of his staff at Combined Operations and an expert on landing craft. At the end of it, he made a facetious reference to 'sardines', which was as good a clue to Sardinia as any German Intelligence officer might hope for. His letter to General Eisenhower accompanied two copies of a booklet which had been published in Britain about Combined Operations – with a request that the General should write a 'message' for the American edition. Its main purpose was to identify its mysterious carrier as a thoroughly responsible officer.

The letters were just right. Nothing was overdone in them. The information was conveyed almost casually. Had it been set down more directly, the Germans might have suspected an intention to deceive. In their friendly style, telling enough but not too much, they were entirely convincing.

It now remained to build up an identity for the body. The Spanish authorities would obviously go through his pockets and it might well be that German agents would have a sight of the contents. By some means, whatever they contained would have to show the dead man as a thoroughly plausible character. It was not enough for the documents to be convincing: the courier had to carry just as much conviction.

At first, they thought of putting him into the Army. On further reflection, however, they decided that the Royal Marines would be better. Army officers did not have to display photographs of themselves on their identity cards, whilst Royal Marines did. If somebody could be found who resembled the dead man: if his picture could be taken and mounted on the card, it would provide a most positive identification. Luckily, somebody could be found. He was photographed, and the snap was stuck into Naval Identity Card No 148228 which purported to have been issued to 'Captain (Acting Major) William Martin' of the Royal Marines. 'Martin' was chosen because there were several men with that name serving as officers in the Marines. 'William', as a Christian name, seemed safe and unobtrusive.

The card recorded that Major Martin was on the staff of Combined Operations: that he had been born in 1907 and

The Life and Death of Major Martin

that his birthplace had been Cardiff. The photograph showed the face of an intelligent man in his early thirties – quiet, perhaps, and even shy at first. It matched up beautifully to the type of person Lord Mountbatten had described in his letter to the Commander-in-Chief, Mediterranean.

But an identity card which has been carried in a man's pocket for goodness knows how long becomes worn in a special sort of way. It is an effect which only time can create. The authors of the plot discovered that, no matter what they did, it obstinately refused to look anything other than dangerously new.

The only solution was to make it clear that this *was* a new one. But why? There could only be one answer: like many other people, Major Martin had *lost* his original identity card. This one, as an endorsement on it showed, was a replacement.

This gave the basic facts about him, but it still did not create a flesh and blood character. A man's pockets contain all manner of odds and ends which, when put together, suggest the kind of person he is. Even such apparently trivial items as bus tickets and old bills, cigarettes and a bunch of keys, help to build up a picture. It was decided that anyone who studied the contents of Major Martin's pockets should be able to build up a satisfactory portrait.

But, first of all, they had to work out what kind of individual it should be. In a great many ways, it was rather like a novelist creating a character. He would obviously have had some money on him at the time, and so they filled his wallet with one five-pound note and three one-pound notes. Into the pockets of his battledress trousers went one half-crown, two shilling pieces, two sixpenny bits and four pennies. He was also provided with two used bus tickets, a box of matches, a packet of cigarettes, a bunch of keys and the stub of a pencil.

So far, these were things which anybody might carry. Now they had to get closer to the major's identity. What kind of a man *was* he? As a serving officer, he might be expected to belong to one of the London clubs which cater for the armed forces. They chose the Naval and Military in Piccadilly, and they enclosed a receipted bill for six nights' accommodation. This was dated April 24th, a few days before the body was due to be discovered, and indicated where he had been staying before he set off on his ill-fated journey. They also included the stubs of two theatre tickets for a popular West End show and an invitation to a nightclub.

Most people, particularly in wartime, have letters in their pockets. The planners decided that Martin might reasonably have become engaged to a young woman, and so they created a fictitious person named Pam. There were two letters from 'Pam', indicating that they had only recently become betrothed; that her parents lived in a country house down in Wiltshire; and that she had a job in some Government department. These were composed by an anonymous young lady and were precisely the kind of things which might have been written under the circumstances. For good measure, a girl at the Admiralty supplied a snapshot of herself, which showed 'Pam' to be a pretty girl, just the sort that a chap like Major Martin might have selected as his bride. And, for even more supporting evidence, the bill for an engagement ring (£53.03) was included.

There was also a letter from the major's 'father', who was portrayed as a rather narrow-minded, distinctly old fashioned, gentleman, who had written to his 'son' while on a visit to his sister, in North Wales. He did not appear to accept the news of the engagement with any great relish.

But this was still not the complete picture. The bank accounts of a good many young officers were overdrawn in wartime, and they decided that Major Martin should be no exception. A letter from the joint general manager of Lloyds Bank pointed out that he was £79.98 in the red, and it was about time he did something about it. The letter closed on the ominous note that, if the major did not act reasonably

The Life and Death of Major Martin

promptly, the bank would have 'no alternative but to take the necessary steps to protect our interests'.

One last thing. A soldier posted overseas in wartime is apt to make his will – especially if he has just become engaged. A letter from a firm of solicitors was enclosed, confirming that this had been done, and that Major Martin had instructed them to include a legacy of £50 to his batman.

All these bills and letters were written on the appropriate notepaper, and many of them were genuine documents. For example, the joint managing director of the bank actually wrote and signed the letter in question, and the bill for the engagement ring was made out by a highly reputable firm of West End jewellers. Various cover stories had to be produced to obtain these valuable pieces of paper, for the real purpose could obviously not be divulged. But they worked, and Major Martin had now become a thoroughly credible person.

The letters from General Nye and Lord Louis Mountbatten were put into a briefcase, which was strapped to the dead man's wrist. This is a method used by bank messengers, but not by the armed forces. However, it was necessary. How, otherwise, could they have made certain that the documents were related to the dead 'major', and that they were discovered at the same time as his body? In any case, the Germans were unlikely to be worried by such a trifling inaccuracy as this.

The time was now approaching when the evidence would have to be planted. A submarine, HMS *Seraph*, was about to sail from Greenock in Scotland on passage to Malta. The commanding officer, Lt N. A. Jewell, was let into the secret and given a thorough briefing. The corpse, which had been kept in cold storage, was fitted out with battledress. A 'Mae West' was put over his shoulders, his pockets were filled with the details of his life, and the briefcase was attached to one of his wrists. He was put into a special container packed with dry ice, and two men spent a long night on the road, driving him up to Greenock. The canister containing the body was labelled 'Optical Instruments'. The crew of the submarine were told that it was, in fact, a special buoy, which had to be put into the sea off the coast of Spain. Its purpose was to report weather conditions by radio. If the Spanish authorities knew about it, they would remove it – which was a reasonable way of accounting for the 'cloak and dagger' nature of the operation.

Only the submarine's officers were told the true nature of their cargo, and they did not hear about it until the last moment, when Major Martin was dropped overboard on his last journey.

Seraph had an uneventful voyage. After ten days at sea, she surfaced off the south coast of Spain at 4.30 in the morning of April 30th, 1943. There were some Spanish fishing boats in the vicinity, but the nearest was about a mile away. It seemed safe to assume that they had not noticed the submarine.

The sea was calm, the visibility patchy, with low clouds and traces of mist. The canister was taken on deck, and 'Major Martin' was extracted from it by the boat's officers. At a point about 1,600 yards from the mouth of the Huelva River, the major, with his 'Mae West' blown up, was gently committed to the water. A rubber dinghy, such as might be used in the event of an aircraft disaster, was also put overboard – upside down and with only one paddle.

HMS *Seraph* withdrew from the scene, submerged and continued her voyage to Malta. The British part of 'Operation Mincemeat' had been completed. The rest depended upon the Spanish authorities and the Germans.

It all went magnificently according to plan. A Spanish fisherman discovered the corpse that very same morning. It was taken on board a launch and carried ashore, where it was handed over to a Spanish naval patrol. There was never any news of the dinghy which, presumably, was too valuable a prize to be handed over to the authorities.

A Spanish fisherman discovered the corpse that very same morning

Presently, news of Major Martin's discovery was sent to the British Embassy in Madrid – along with his personal effects. The 'secret documents' were returned a few days later. When they reached the Admiralty in London, the experts were able to tell that somebody had tampered with them. The authors of 'Operation Mincemeat' were content. This could only mean that copies had been made and, presumably, had been sent to Berlin. Provided the German High Command took them sufficiently seriously, all would be well.

'Major Martin' was buried with full honours in the graveyard at Huelva. His death was announced in the newspapers, and that was that. It was not until the end of the war, that the true measure of the operation's success became clear. Captured German documents showed that the letters from Nye and Mountbatten had been examined at the highest possible level, and that even Hitler had studied them. What is even more important, the German High Command was completely convinced that there would be no large scale invasion of Sicily. They swallowed the information so delicately conveyed, and made haste to reinforce their units in Greece.

The identity of the dead man who played the part of Major Martin has never been revealed, but it is fair to say that the operation in which he unwittingly took part saved a great many British and American lives. Perhaps, unknowingly, he was one of the heroes of World War II.

To find a dead man playing the part of an impostor is rare. More commonly, it is the living who do these things. If Major Martin exemplifies the former, it would be difficult to find any better example of the latter than the strange mission of Lt M. E. Clifton James: a peacetime actor, who was serving in the British Army, and who bore a quite remarkable resemblance to Field-Marshal Montgomery.

The year was 1944. The invasion of Sicily was over and

The Life and Death of Major Martin

done with. Allied forces were firmly established in Italy and were pressing northwards. Plans for the landings in France were nearing completion. The Germans were in no doubt that such an operation would take place, but they had no idea of where it would be. The more that could be done to mystify them, the better.

One possibility was that North Africa might be the launching pad, and that the assaults would be made on beaches in the South of France. The advantage from the Allied point of view would be that this area was less strongly defended than the Channel coast. Although there were many things to be said against it, the Germans might conceivably swallow such an idea; and, for this reason, Plan 303 was conceived.

The essence of it was that Montgomery should make a trip to Gibraltar and Algiers, where he would meet prominent British and American military leaders and, during the course of his conversations, let fall certain remarks which would point to the South of France as the objective. With a bit of luck they would be picked up by the receptive ears of enemy agents and be reported back to Germany. Gibraltar was likely to be a particularly happy hunting ground for, as in the case of Major Martin, there were a number of Spaniards there who were known to be sympathetic to the German cause.

The thing, of course, was that the distinguished visitor would not be the Field-Marshal at all. He was busy enough in Britain, without making quick visits to the Mediterranean to distribute false clues. Fortunately, however, his presence was not necessary. Provided he was coached carefully in Montgomery's habits, his way of speech, and so on, Lt Clifton Jones would do just as well. The fact that he not only looked like the Field-Marshal, but was also an actor by trade, was a particularly happy coincidence. By his stage craft, he would be able to master the role much more quickly and competently than the average individual.

Before setting out, he spent a day down in the South of England, accompanying the Field-Marshal wherever he went. His eyes and his ears greedily absorbed the details; and, by the time he was suitably fitted out in a replica of Montgomery's uniform, it was very difficult to tell the difference. He not only spoke like Montgomery: he even began to *think* like him.

One evening, a few weeks before 'D' Day, Clifton James boarded an aircraft at Northolt Aerodrome near London and flew to Gibraltar. After landing, he was greeted by the Governor. During a stroll in the grounds of Government House after lunch, the two men discussed fictitious meetings of the War Cabinet in Britain, and made particular reference to 'Plan 303'. This, if it had ever existed, would have been the code word for the phoney invasion. They were not alone at the time, and the Governor was able to point out at least two Spaniards who were known to be German agents and who, on some pretext or other, had reason to be there.

Things went equally well in North Africa. Before very long, the authorities in Berlin were exhorting all their secret servicemen to find out more about 'Plan 303'. Eventually, the man who was mistaken for Montgomery flew back to Britain from Cairo. His mission, it was agreed, had been most successful.

It was not until after the war that Clifton James knew how close he had come to disaster. When the German High Command heard about the proposed trip of the man who was thought to be Montgomery, they gave orders that his aircraft was to be shot down. If that failed, he was to be assassinated during his stay in North Africa. But, at the last minute, Hitler himself intervened. No attempts were to be made on the Field-Marshal's life, he insisted, until more information about the invasion plans had been collected. Thanks partly to Clifton James' work as impostor, it never was.

10

The Improbable Paintings

It was late one afternoon in 1937. The air in the studio was thick with cigarette smoke, and the light was fading. Hans van Meegeren turned away from his easel and walked over to a table in a corner of the room. He poured out a glass of wine. Taking a long drink, he gazed at the painting he had just completed. Then he slumped down in a chair. He was tired beyond all imagining.

The picture was a masterpiece – there was no doubt about that. It showed Christ talking with his disciples at Emmaus. Nobody who was familiar with van Meegeren's work would have guessed that he had produced it.

According to his critics, his output was lacking in taste and had about as much subtlety as a steam hammer. This was different. It possessed beauty, harmony, power. Everything about it was faultless. It might very well have been painted by that Dutch master of the seventeenth century, Jan Vermeer. Indeed, unless van Meegeren's plan went disastrously wrong, nobody would ever know that it had *not* been painted by Vermeer.

Would anybody ever discover the truth? He doubted it. He had been at endless pains to make his deception perfect, and it certainly hadn't been easy. It is one thing to make a picture in the manner of an Old Master. It is quite another to do it in such a way that it will fool the experts. It not only has to *look* old: if it is to survive the tests which can prove or disprove its authenticity, it must somehow *be* old.

After many experiments, van Meegeren had found a way of producing this effect by baking the finished painting in an oven. But that had only been part of the problem. Before Vermeer got to work on a picture, he did not, simply, call in at his local supplier and buy a few tubes of paint. It wasn't nearly so easy in his day: he more or less had to make the stuff himself. Van Meegeren had studied every masterpiece the Dutch Master had ever done. But that wasn't enough. He had also carried out a secret investigation into seventeenth-century methods of paint-making. He had found that Vermeer was in the habit of using an ultramarine made from lapis lazuli. It was hard to come by, and a single tube had cost him something in the region of £200. And those vivid crimsons – they came from the crushed shells of a female insect that is only found in Mexico. White lead and, even, earth were other materials he used in his attempts to deceive the eyes and the apparatus of the experts.

Even the canvas was of the right period. Originally, a rather dull work by a very minor master had been painted on it. Van Meegeren had ruthlessly obliterated it with his own composition. If anything could make people believe that an unknown Vermeer had been discovered, this would be it.

In all, 'The Man of Emmaus' (as he decided to call the picture) had taken seven months of hard work to produce. It had all been done in complete secrecy, and not even his wife was allowed into his studio. Now, he had just to bake the canvas carefully and the first part of his plan would be complete.

Why was he going to so much trouble? The reason, he supposed, was the art critics. He bitterly resented the scorn they showed for his own paintings. Admittedly, the public did not seem to share their views. They bought his pictures and now, at forty-seven years of age, he was moderately wealthy. He could afford to rent this studio in the South of France many miles from his native Holland. He could live in a certain amount of style. Perhaps he ought to be contented. Money, surely, was what everything was about. That was what those fat Dutch businessmen, whose portraits he sometimes painted, told him. Well – he had made plenty of that. Surely it was enough?

But he knew that it was not. Deep down inside himself, he realized that the critics were right. He would never have admitted it, but it rankled. Perhaps, by producing a masterpiece that everybody would mistake for a Vermeer, he would show them how much ability he really had. The only trouble was that, if he succeeded, he would have to keep the secret to himself. Nobody, apart from himself, would ever know that van Meegeren, the popular artist whom the experts derided, had the talents of an Old Master. Indeed, it was for this very reason that he had chosen this particular genius as his inspiration. During his lifetime, Vermeer himself had been badly treated by the critics. There should, perhaps, be a fellow-feeling between them.

If the secret ever came out, he might, he supposed, be accused of forgery, but the word was totally inappropriate. This was not a copy of a Vermeer painting. It was an entirely original work carried out in the master's style. The very fact that he had done it surely gave him title to take his place with the greatest artists of all time? The whole thing was so far removed from the area of petty crime, that it was not worth thinking about.

It was now dark in the studio. Van Meegeren put down his empty glass and squashed out the umpteenth cigarette of the day. He gave a final glance in the direction of his masterpiece, and went outside – carefully locking the door behind him.

Some while later, a Dutch lawyer was on a visit to Paris. One of his clients, an eminent businessman, had died and his task was to wind up the estate. Among the contents of the dead man's apartment was a painting showing Christ with his disciples at Emmaus. It was covered in dust.

'That's a nice picture,' the lawyer said.

'You like it?' the widow said. 'We've never cared for it very much. We've only had it for about a year. I can't remember how my husband got hold of it.'

'Would you mind if I borrowed it for a short while?'

'You can keep it, if you like. I'm sure we don't want it.'

The lawyer packed up the painting carefully and, as soon as his business was done, he sent a telegram to his office in Amsterdam. He would be away longer than he had expected, he told them. A sudden change of plan compelled him to visit the South of France.

Armed with the painting, he presently arrived in Monte Carlo, where he had an appointment with one of Europe's most distinguished art collectors. He already had a theory about what, to his mind at any rate, was a very important discovery. This man would be able to say whether he was right or wrong.

In the quiet of his host's library, he unwrapped 'The Man of Emmaus' and placed it against a wall. 'Tell me,' he said, 'what do you think of this?'

The collector studied it in silence. Then he turned to the lawyer with a look of intense excitement on his face. 'It is superb,' he said. 'A masterpiece. This, my friend, is a wonderful moment in my life. Let me just make sure of one more thing.'

Picking up a magnifying glass, he went up to the picture and examined it in greater detail.

'Do you realize what you have here?' he asked.

'I hardly dare believe it,' the lawyer said.

'There is no doubt at all about it. Look at those initials. "J.V.M.". Do you understand what they stand for? "Vermeer." There can be no doubt that this is a genuine *Vermeer*. They can test it in any way they like: you will not be disappointed. However did you come across it?'

The lawyer told him.

The Improbable Paintings

'Fools!' the collector muttered. 'They must have been blind. This is no ordinary Vermeer: it is the master at the top of his form, and even breaking new ground. I cannot tell you how important this is, and I cannot thank you enough for bringing it to me.'

Back in Amsterdam, the lawyer sold the painting to the city's leading museum for £50,000. Soon afterwards, it was exhibited in a show entitled 'Masterpieces of Four Centuries', and everyone was enraptured with it. Like the expert at Monte Carlo, they agreed that this was not just another Vermeer which had been uncovered, but one of the greatest works he had ever produced.

During the next few years, a number of other unknown Vermeers were brought to light and so were two by that artist's contemporary, Pieter de Hooch. They were mostly concerned with Biblical themes and, like 'The Man of Emmaus', they were all examples of the artist at his formidable best. Indeed, they revealed a new aspect of his work: as if he had extended himself beyond the range of landscapes and portraits for which he was more generally known, and had set out to explore a deeper, more mystical world.

Meanwhile, war had broken out and van Meegeren had returned to Amsterdam, where he was now living in a large house in the centre of the city. He seemed to be remarkably well off, but this was hardly surprising. His own painting was enjoying a boom. It was just the type of thing which the Germans and their Dutch collaborators liked. Even Hitler was said to be a fan of the small, hard-drinking and heavy-smoking Dutch artist. When a book containing reproductions of his pictures was published, an autographed copy was sent to the German leader.

In addition to the financial success of his painting, he also appeared to be enjoying a run of luck in quite another direction. He regularly bought tickets in the national lottery and, by all accounts, was winning big prizes.

Van Meegeren continued to be associated by the experts with a style of painting which was bad art but good business. Few people knew that he was also behind the discoveries of the works by Vermeer. He was acting as a kind of middle man. Somewhere in Italy, the story went, there was a noble family which had fallen upon hard times. To make ends meet, they had been compelled to sell their priceless collection of masterpieces, and had entrusted this task to their friend Hans van Meegeren. They were proud people who felt that it was disgraceful to be poor. Van Meegeren could do what he liked with their Vermeers, provided he obtained the best possible prices for them, and provided he never revealed their owners' identity.

It was not difficult to obey both these conditions. The art world of Europe was much too excited about the discoveries to care very much about *where* they came from. Nor was it hard to sell them for large sums of money. They were, after all, *beyond* price.

Shortly after the Nazi conquest of Holland, a German banker had moved to Amsterdam and taken over one of the city's art galleries. Van Meegeren and he were on the best of terms, and it was through the former that the banker was introduced to a Vermeer discovery entitled 'Christ and the Adulteress'. The German was in no doubt about how to dispose of it. Back in his own country, there was a Nazi leader whose appetite for works of art was insatiable. His name was Hermann Göring. Göring, he believed, would pay anything to get his hands on the painting. Van Meegeren was given a cheque for about £150,000. The picture was crated up, and dispatched to Göring's home near Berlin.

The war came to an end. The German banker left Holland hurriedly and took up residence in Spain. Van Meegeren waited, a little uneasily, perhaps, for whatever was in store for him. It was not long in coming. The little artist had been on much too friendly terms with the Nazi authorities. Had

The Improbable Paintings

not a copy of his book been discovered in Hitler's library? Had he not helped to rob Holland of one of her rightful masterpieces, when he made it possible for Göring to acquire 'Christ and the Adulteress'? He was, and there was no other word for it, a traitor: a man who had grown rich by selling works of art to the Nazis.

In due course, he was arrested and brought to trial. It was at this point that he decided to reveal the truth. When asked about the Vermeer which had been delivered to Göring, he simply said: '*What* Vermeer?' He explained to the court that he had painted it himself – just as he had painted all the other 'discoveries'. He also pointed out that the Italian family was a complete fabrication, made up by himself, to account for the pictures. Holland had just as many real Vermeers as ever that nation had possessed. Those which had been exported were brilliant fakes, done so well that even the experts had been deceived.

The court was unable to believe his testimony. This, surely, was impossible. There had never been any doubts about the authenticity of the pictures. How could he expect anybody to believe that they were impostors?

'I will show you,' van Meegeren said. 'If you allow me to return to my studio, I will paint a "Vermeer" for you, and you will be able to see how it was done. Tell me what subject you would like, and I will do it.'

It must have been one of the strangest interludes that any court of law has ever produced. Van Meegeren was allowed to return to his studio. With him went the judges, a guard of policemen, and a professor or two as expert witnesses. When he asked what he should paint, they suggested that young Jesus teaching in the temple might be a suitable subject. Then they sat back, eager to enjoy what they imagined was going to be a most embarrassing situation. Vermeer! How could this small upstart, with his heavy handed approach to art, produce anything even resembling a real Vermeer – let alone a masterpiece which would fool the art world's great experts?

Van Meegeren worked away quietly, smoking his endless chain of cigarettes and helping himself lavishly to tots of Dutch gin. Now and again, he muttered something to himself. That was the only thing which broke the silence of the

Van Meegeren worked away quietly ...

studio – that and his heavy breathing and the occasional scrape of a match or the rattle of a glass.

The judges and the professors began to marvel. If there were going to be a joke, it looked as if it would be on them. The composition which was steadily revealing itself on the canvas had nothing to do with the laboured art of van Meegeren. It *was* a Vermeer. Technically it would have delighted the master himself: indeed, sometimes it was hard to

The Improbable Paintings

imagine that the little man who was working away so intently was the suspected German collaborator Hans van Meegeren. It might so easily have been Vermeer.

Eventually, the picture was finished. 'There,' van Meegeren said – not without a touch of pride in his voice. 'Can I show you anything else?'

'You can show us how it is done,' one of the professors said.

Van Meegeren showed them. He taught them how he produced his colours – not by the twentieth-century method but in the manner that Vermeer had used nearly 300 years earlier. He turned out a cupboard, which was packed with properties such as swords and dishes and items of clothing, all of which had appeared in the supposed 'discoveries'. He described to them the picture on top of which he had painted 'The Man of Emmaus', and X-ray tests revealed that he was speaking the truth.

The professors and the judges were convinced. Van Meegeren could no longer stand trial for helping the Nazis, for he had hoaxed them magnificently. Even so, justice had not yet done with him. He had made a great deal of money out of his so-called Vermeers, and it might well be argued that he had committed some sort of forgery. He was brought to court again on a charge of deception.

On this occasion, the courtroom looked more like a picture gallery. All the 'Vermeers' were there – plus the two 'De Hooch' paintings. The prosecutor demanded that van Meegeren should be sent to prison for two years. The judges were more lenient. They decided that one year would be enough, and they clearly reflected public opinion. He had scarcely been sentenced before a movement was started to secure his release. He himself told newspaper men that he would take his punishment as 'a good sport'.

Alas – he died in that same year. In some ways, it was as if this small, nervous, reckless man had burned himself out.

Or, perhaps, his work was done. Not only had he shown the critics that he could paint just as well as an acknowledged master: he had been compelled by circumstances to show the world at large that this was so. The long-dead Vermeer no longer had the credit for these magnificent paintings. At last, ten years after 'The Man of Emmaus', the extent of van Meegeren's genius was realized.